MICHAEL BRAY

Michael Bray trained as an actor at the Royal Academy of Dramatic Art, before working in theatre, television and film as an actor, including six years at the National Theatre, where he also wrote and directed his first two plays, *The Rhythm of Love* and *The Back of the Bus Girls* at the National Theatre Studio.

He then moved into writing and directing for television and film. He wrote and directed *The Sea Change*, which was chosen for the Sundance Film Festival, and starred Ray Winstone, Maryam d'Abo and Sean Chapman. After that, he joined Winchester Films and worked on numerous films including *The Killing Joke*, *Black Powder* (Ealing Films), *The Possession of Julie May* (Gaumont) and *The Commitments 2*, and his screenplay for *Maggie* won the Producers Alliance Award in 2004. Most recently in 2018, Michael was Executive Producer on *Where the Skin Lies* for Signwriter Films, which had successful distribution in America and has been screened at major film festivals worldwide, and is an executive producer and board member of Dog Star Films.

Michael is currently Course Leader of MA Screen, Acting and MA Screen, Directing, Writing, the film-making courses at Drama Centre, Central Saint Martins, part of the University of the Arts London. He also teaches screen acting at Guildhall School of Music & Drama. He was Head of Film and Television for Arts Educational Schools London, and then Director of the School of Acting for nine years, creating and directing over three hundred films that were screened at BAFTA in London, New York and Los Angeles. He also created a range of new film courses at ArtsEd including the first BA in Film Acting in the UK.

Other titles in this series

SO YOU WANT TO ACT ON SCREEN?

Michael Bray

NICK HERN BOOKS

London

www.nickhernbooks.co.uk

A Nick Hern Book

SO YOU WANT TO BE A SCREEN ACTOR?
first published in Great Britain in 2019
by Nick Hern Books Limited
The Glasshouse, 49a Goldhawk Road, London W12 8QP

Cover image: Shutterstock.com/Barbol

Designed and typeset by Nick Hern Books, London
Printed and bound in Great Britain by
Ashford Colour Press, Gosport, Hampshire

A CIP catalogue record for this book
is available from the British Library

ISBN 978 1 84842 071 7

MIX
Paper from
responsible sources
FSC
www.fsc.org   FSC® C011748

To Sara, Gabriel and Rose

Contents

PART TWO: PRACTICE

Introduction

Screen versus Stage

What makes one screen performance better than another? Why are Al Pacino's screen performances so fascinating? What makes his characters bristle with energy? How does Kate Winslet reveal her thoughts so clearly to the audience? What makes Cate Blanchett so believable? Cary Grant so charming? George Clooney so likeable? Tom Hardy so sexy?

There are any number of actors who are unique and talented but somehow have not fulfilled their potential in front of the camera and, similarly, many whose great stage careers simply haven't transferred to the screen. Why is this? In part because they lack the screen-acting techniques that would let their talent shine through; the basic skills that would enable them to give the screen performances of which they are truly capable.

I trained as an actor thirty years ago and had a successful career in theatre, film and television before moving into directing film, so I've seen this from both sides of the camera. I've worked both with brilliant screen actors and, of course, good actors who just didn't cut it in front of the camera.

So what made the difference? Their *process*. The process they go through to achieve a performance and the techniques they employ to reveal it to the camera. Sadly, in many cases it's a lack of technique that is revealed.

When I began my acting career there was little or no training for the screen. There still isn't enough. The accepted wisdom was that an actor learned to act, then adapted those skills for screen acting. It was only when I started directing film that I realised this assumption was nonsense. While you're actually filming, there's little or no time to teach an actor the basics. Nor do you want to have to coax a performance from them as you would in the theatre. You need actors who can arrive on set having done all the necessary preparation, so that their character is fully rounded and ready to be revealed on screen. You need actors who understand the rhythm of film-making, who can enter the world of the character completely, despite being surrounded on all sides by equipment and crew.

So I started to analyse what it is that makes a good screen performance, and how it can be achieved. What I discovered is that actors have to make some simple but profound changes to the way they approach their craft, the text and their preparation.

This book will give you a clear insight into the art of screen acting, enabling you to deliver performances that will both satisfy you as a creative artist and impress industry professionals, so that they want to employ you again. The book contains exercises and observations that will help you avoid basic errors in your preparation and guide you towards creating exciting, real characters that you can deliver on professional film sets, under the exacting time pressure that today's industry places on the actor.

The book is designed to be read from beginning to end as a step-by-step guide to the art of screen acting, although those who wish to tackle particular acting problems can just dip into it, as can those who have done a number of film and television jobs but feel that they could have done better or want to re-examine their own methods. The exercises can be done easily at home with a video camera or just on a smartphone. You will also need a friend to be your camera operator, preferably someone you can trust not to burst out laughing as you work. Starting to learn the basics of camera craft away from the pressured environment of a studio or a film location will help you tremendously, but for much of the work you will need only yourself, a notebook and your own insight. Remember, this work is not to be viewed by anyone other than yourself. It's a learning tool, not a showreel, so don't worry too much about location and lighting, or quality of picture: that's not the point. The important thing is that you can see the action you have shot clearly.

All the exercises have been designed for single-camera shooting, which means that each angle of the scene is shot with one camera. Consequently, the scene is repeated many times and might even be shot out of sequence, depending how the camera is being moved. Multi-camera work is closer to theatre, in that you will run a scene through and it is then shot by three or more cameras, which are positioned and moved to follow the blocking of the scene. Some television companies still use this system, mostly for soap operas and the occasional comedy programme, but it's relatively rare these days.

Single-camera shooting, then, is the standard method for both film and television drama, the major differences between the two being time and money. On a big-budget film you might shoot between two and five minutes of footage a day. On a typical television series, however, you would shoot around eight to twelve minutes of useable footage, and some television series film as many as twenty pages in a day. The number of pages shot varies enormously. A lot of low-budget films shoot as much footage in a day as television, and many big television series – especially those currently being made by companies like HBO, Sky, Netflix and Amazon – are much closer in their daily ratio to big-budget films. The shooting process is much the same, some are just shot much more quickly than others. A film will probably do fewer 'set-ups' than television, so there's more sitting around, whereas in television you will be shooting constantly and mostly in mid-shot, with lots more dialogue.

More about all this later, but for now let's just begin by considering the basics...

What is screen acting, and is it really any different from stage acting? Well, yes, it's almost completely different. Although stage and screen acting have the same root, in that you are trying to make a character as real as possible within the world created by the writer – as Sanford Meisner said, 'living truthfully under imagined circumstances' – the process by which you arrive at a performance, and the environment in which you deliver it, are so different as to be virtually two distinct art forms. Let's compare these differences.

The most fundamental difference is the process you go through in creating a performance. Stage acting is *linear* and *organic*. The process begins on day one with a read-through of the script, and after that you, the other actors and the director are in a private rehearsal space, working together towards the first night. Good, bad or indifferent, you have shared the creative process; you have watched each others' performances develop over the weeks of rehearsal. You are focused on, and share together in, the terrifying pleasure of the first night. When you walk on stage at the beginning of the performance you know what your fellow actors are going to do. You all start at the beginning and move in a direct narrative line towards the end of the play, knowing how and when to build to the play's climax. In theatre, the audience are very much a part of the stage performance: they imagine the play along with the actors. As the late director Sir Peter Hall said, 'Theatre is the last place left in our society where people imagine together.'

When Romeo and Juliet lie in bed at the end of Act Three and discuss whether Juliet heard the nightingale or the lark, the audience does not need to see the first glimmers of sunrise creeping through the window. Shakespeare has conveyed all this through the dialogue. The stage actor uses this shared imaginative energy to complete the illusion.

The experience of an actor on a film set, however, is completely different. Screen acting is *non-linear* and *non-organic*, and in that single phrase lies the crucial difference of approach. To begin with, the script is usually shot out of sequence, and you don't get to do detailed rehearsals with the other actors before you shoot your scenes. You may shoot the scene where you leave your husband before the scene in which he proposes to you. You might start the shoot with a passionate bed scene, making love to an actor you only met a few hours earlier. You might kill someone before you meet them.

Because of ever-tighter budgets, hardly any film or television directors get the luxury of rehearsals. So no matter what you had in mind when you were preparing your role at home, it's very likely that the actors with whom you are playing your scenes are completely different from the way you imagined them. Their portrayal of the role and delivery of the lines will be quite different from what you had envisaged. You have to be adaptable and make it work. After all, it will be your face on the screen. If you give a wooden performance – especially in speedily shot television – the viewers won't blame the director for getting the casting of the other parts wrong. They'll just think you weren't very good.

So, acting on screen you don't have the advantage of a shared rehearsal period, or the help of the audience's imagination. You arrive on the film set having never seen what the other actors are doing. You've done all the preparation and character development on your own. Every choice you have made, you have made alone, until the moment that you reveal your character to the director and the rest of the crew at the start of the shoot. That's the harsh reality of screen acting today.

Film and television acting demands enormous courage if you are to succeed. You have to be brave to be good. And to be brave, you need to know what you're doing.

That is the purpose of this book: to offer techniques on how to prepare your performance for the screen, how to deliver it on the day and how to sustain it over a long shoot or television series.

Summary

- The difference between screen acting and theatre is the process:

  Theatre is *linear* and *organic*.

  Screen is *non-linear* and *non-organic*.

- 'Acting is living truthfully under imagined circumstances.'

Acknowledgements

Thanks to all actors featured in the photographs in this book, including Benjamin Adnams, Elizabet Altube, Louisa Boscawen, Frances Brennand Roper, Joshua Diffley, Colin James, Joshua MacLennan, George Phail, Luke Pickett and Mathias Swann; photographs by Mark Duffield and Robert Hamilton.

Scenes from *Gosford Park* by Julian Fellowes, based on an idea by Robert Altman and Bob Balaban, copyright © 2001 USA Films, LLC, published and reproduced by permission of Nick Hern Books Ltd.

PART ONE

Process

The Six Myths of Screen Acting

Socrates wrote that 'It is by finding out what something is not that one comes closest to understanding what it is.' To understand what good screen acting is, we first have to discover what it isn't. There are some very common myths about how you do it:

- Screen acting is 'smaller' than stage acting.

- You only need to think a thought and the camera will see it in your eyes.

- Screen acting is easier than stage acting because you are in the location that fits the scene and you will find it easier to be natural.

- Because you do a lot of takes you are bound to get a good performance.

- You need to do less with your face and body.

- You are less nervous because no one is watching you.

These are the most common assumptions about screen acting – and all of them are wrong. Not only are they wrong, but they can jeopardise a screen career. Through repetition these half-truths have become accepted facts, and by damaging the way screen acting is approached, they can make good actors give bad screen performances.

I'm going to tackle these assumptions head-on and explain why they are wrong, so that we have a clearer picture of what makes good screen acting.

Myth 1: Screen acting is smaller than stage acting

Lots of actors talk about toning down their work for the screen; 'pulling it in', 'making it more internal'. Basically, this manifests itself in them doing less. Terrified of doing too much, they end up doing far too little and risk making their performance flat and boring.

But the oversized performances that they fear belong to another age, when actors were used to playing big theatres that demanded an exaggerated and demonstrative style. Although such acting has fallen out of fashion, modern actors are still aware of its pitfalls and often underplay a role in an effort to appear more 'real' on camera. But by misunderstanding the saying 'less is more', they tend to react passively to what is going on in the scene, and passivity is boring to watch. It's dull for the director to edit and ultimately it's death to a screen career. What really needs to be toned down for screen acting is the vocal level. There's more on this in a later section, but let me state it here at the outset because it's crucial.

The way to avoid these small, cautious performances is to have confidence: make bolder choices whilst being as real as possible. As long as you are being truthful and real, you can forget about the size of the performance. As Marlon Brando said, 'Don't act; be.'

Myth 2: An actor only needs to think the thought and the camera will record it

That you can just think something and the camera will pick it up as if by magic is an odd idea but, again, widely believed. And, again, it's not true. I've heard any number of actors explaining that they are thinking complex and well-researched thoughts. I don't doubt that they are, but unfortunately the camera can't see it.

You have to reveal your character's thoughts to the camera, and to do this you have both to understand the process of film-making and know how to prepare and structure your thinking. Later on I'll give you a number of exercises to improve your ability to reveal your thoughts to camera. Remember Ingmar Bergman's words: 'The camera is not a mirror. The camera doesn't reflect. It reveals.'

Myth 3: Location gives the actor greater reality

The location may be nothing like the one intended in the script. I once shot a judge's summing-up in the stairwell of a London pub because the wooden panelling looked like a courtroom and the production company could not afford a real court for such a small insert. The actor had to make the situation real through his performance. The location looked great on camera but it did little to help him: he was wearing a wig and judge's gown but he was still sitting on the floor of a pub.

Even if the location fits the scene perfectly, the way the scene is shot may take away any advantage this gives the actor. Pub scenes frequently throw up this problem. The way people would sit together naturally does not work for the camera, so actors find themselves being asked to cheat themselves slightly to the left or lean in a bit, until they are perched in positions that are far from natural or comfortable but look real on the camera. And all that interesting background of people chatting, drinking and laughing, everything that gives the scene so much authenticity, is actually shot in total silence, the extras miming their conversation and laughter. The sound that gives the scene such truth is all added later. In reality, you'd be sitting awkwardly at the bar, trying to look relaxed and real, surrounded by an enormous and intimidating film crew, a microphone inches from your head, and a piece of polystyrene reflecting light into your eyes.

At such moments an actor can only achieve reality through deep concentration. You must be able to project yourself into the world of the character completely, whilst monitoring your own performance and remaining creatively open to the other actors – all this and still be able to absorb the director's notes. This is quite a feat and can only be achieved by practised concentration.

The great James Dean said that acting is 'pure concentration'. We will explore in later sections how to expand your power of concentration and enter the world of the character more easily.

Myth 4: Many takes will ensure a good screen performance

Directors do many takes of a scene but this is not only to allow the actor to get it right. The director expects you to be line-perfect and ready to step into character on arrival. The first few takes might be lost because of sound issues or problems with background action, or maybe the camera is moving during the scene and it takes time to coordinate the crew.

What the director wants is for you to be totally convincing in character right from the first take. He wants to mould your performance, not have to coax it out of you. Nothing is more frustrating than watching an actor struggling to produce a performance. Once you reach take six or seven, and you're still missing the emotional truth of the scene (or worse, fluffing lines), the pressure will start to crush any talent or confidence you had. You struggle with even the most basic moments of the scene. At this point the director and the producers will be starting to think about recasting. On film and in television you have no time to develop a performance: you must arrive with the character fully formed and ready to adapt to any situation that the director throws at you.

Later sections will deal extensively with the right level of preparation and relaxation needed to deal with the pressure of a modern film set. But let's be clear that the more preparation you do, the more relaxed you will be on the day. Lots of actors, out of fear and ignorance, quickly learn their lines and hope they can wing it on the day.

But Spencer Tracy got it right when he said, 'Once I get on set I just have to say the lines and hit my marks. The real work is done before I get there.'

Myth 5: Screen acting means doing less with your face and body

Believing that the camera can read their minds, actors do little or nothing with their bodies or faces, concentrating most of the character into the intonation of their voices. This is fine in most theatre productions, where the narrative is driven by dialogue, but it's of no use in film. Screen acting is driven by thought, and each separate thought affects your breathing – and consequently your body – in some way, and that includes the face. Just watch how animated real people's faces are, how they struggle to keep their thoughts and emotions from showing.

So it should be for the film actor. Rather than keeping your face blank, you should regard it as a canvas on which to reveal or hide the character's thoughts. Your body should be free to reveal your character's thinking, as opposed to being a repressed bundle of fear or passive neutrality.

As long as the reactions are driven by real thoughts, every-thing you do will be believable. More importantly, you'll be giving the director material to work with in the edit. Far too often directors sit in the edit suite searching through the rushes for a reaction to cut to, only to discover that the actors have neutralised their facial reactions and body lan-guage and that they have nothing to work with.

In film and television drama, you need to reveal the inner thinking of your character, reacting and then suppressing reactions to the other characters and the situation. Things that the stage actor might think of as 'upstaging' – because they would draw attention away from the other actors as they were speaking – are absolutely necessary in screen act-ing. But you need the skill and knowledge to know when and how to do it. Keeping your face neutral and body tense loses you precious screen time.

As director Steven Spielberg remarked, 'Acting is reacting.'

Myth 6: Nerves are easier to overcome in screen acting because there are fewer people watching

Nonsense. A film or a television set can be very, very fright-ening. You will arrive on set on your first day to discover that the crew have a camaraderie that you don't yet share. Unless you are the star, to them you'll be just another actor. Because you are passing through, they will be polite but won't spend a great deal of effort trying to get to know you. The director, who you last saw at the casting or perhaps at the read-through, is busy shooting so will pay you little attention until you are actually called onto the set.

The second assistant director will take you to your trailer or dressing room. You get into your costume for the scene you are about to shoot and then you wait. You could be waiting for hours. Being a screen actor can be very isolating, and the isolation creates an echo chamber for all your doubts.

Then you are called to the set. You shake hands with the other actors, whom you have probably never met before. The director, always pressed for time, says, 'Right, let's have a stumble through the scene, shall we?'

The tone is always easy and casual, but don't let that fool you. A lot happens when you first run a scene; many important decisions will be made about how it will be shot. If you are nervous, the bold, brilliant decisions you thought you would make when you were working on the script at home will suddenly shrink into safe, cautious choices.

The director will then shape the scene, giving you your blocking and the rhythm and temperature of the scene. Then the director of photography will start lighting the scene in the shooting order that the director and first assistant director have agreed on.

You will be taken to make-up. Then you sit in your trailer/dressing room, made up and in costume, waiting to do your scene. Perhaps for hours.

Finally you are called onto the set and then, for the first time, you are at the very centre of the storm. The first assistant director shouts for quiet, and everybody on and around the set goes silent. The art department stop moving props and bits of set, the technicians stop joking, turn and stare. The director, the director of photography, and maybe twenty other people are watching.

Can you do it? Trust me, even the most experienced stars get nervous when they walk onto a film set.

What you need to learn is how to handle your nerves properly, so that they don't hinder your performance. Learn how to focus your preparation, so that when you step into that vulnerable and exposed place in front of the camera, you can use the pressure to excel. By controlling your fear, you will make bolder choices when you first run the scene and not limit yourself to timid, self-conscious choices. You must learn to see the crew not as the enemy but as people who can help you realise your vision of the character. 'The thing that screen actors need above everything else is confidence,' observed director Sidney Lumet.

Summary

- Screen acting is not smaller, just more concentrated and driven by thought. Vocal levels are a lot lower than on stage. Be in the moment as the character.

- The camera is not a magic device that can read your mind. You have to reveal your thoughts to it.

- Location is rarely a help to the actor. You have to be totally concentrated on set or in the location because you'll be surrounded by technicians and equipment.

- You do not get many takes to get your performance right. There are a lot of things to be coordinated in a scene, so you have to be the character, in the moment, from the first take onwards.

- Don't forget that your face and body are crucial in revealing your thoughts on screen. Do not become a talking head, relying on your voice for the whole performance. Stay connected to your centre.

- Being on set is quite frightening. The more *prepared* you are, the better you'll be at controlling your nerves.

Now that we've dismissed those common myths, we can move on to what screen acting really is. We'll start with an exercise.

Exercise: The Dead Body

This exercise looks easy but it embraces all the fundamentals of screen acting. The scene has no dialogue and the action is very clear. Couldn't be simpler.

We will go back to this exercise throughout the book, so you'll be able to see your improvement as you learn the techniques.

THE SCENE. 'The Body in the Kitchen'

Fade in.

Home from work, Leslie enters the kitchen. Stops by the doorway, aware that there is something on the floor. A dead body. Realising someone's been murdered, Leslie runs out of the kitchen.

CUT.

Clearly this is an extreme event, but not at all uncommon in the world of film and television. Done well, the scene can lead the viewer into a great story; done badly it will just seem vaguely comic or, worse, absurd.

It's important at this stage in the learning process that you don't judge yourself too harshly. Remember: you have to get it wrong to get it right.

That is why we do these exercises. If watching your first efforts just makes you throw your hands up in horror, you will simply close up as an artist and ultimately you'll learn nothing.

Normally I would be beside the student actor when they review their work, pointing out what works and what doesn't. I know from experience that it's better to point out what works rather than emphasise the negative. Obviously I can't do that here, so I am relying on you to be objective but not overly critical. Look for what's good. Once you see what doesn't work on screen, you can concentrate on what does work for you. And remember, no one will see this work except you and your camera operator. A good screen actor has to have a positive mindset.

So now I want you to set up the camera in your kitchen. Place it as far from the door as possible. Place a mark (a cross of tape) on the floor, just to the right of the camera. That's your eyeline for the dead body. Now leave the room and when your camera operator shouts 'Action!', I want you to enter the kitchen, see the dead body and then leave.

It would be best if you did the exercise now, without reading on to my round-up of the techniques – and the common mistakes – it involves.

I know from experience that this exercise exposes the following common mistakes:

Your reaction on seeing the body is too small

How do I know? Because most actors monitor the size of their reaction and are frightened of doing too much, so consequently their reactions are much too small. Especially to something as momentous as finding a dead body. Terrified of being melodramatic, you do far too little.

You entered the room looking serious

Many actors generalise in a scene like this. Because you are about to see a dead body, which is a shocking and tragic event, you approach the scene seriously, pre-empting the fact that you are about to see a dead body. That transmits into your attitude toward the scene, so you enter the room looking intense and serious. What you should do is enter the scene with an entirely different mindset, a mental attitude totally different from the one that you will end the scene with. To put it crudely, if you end the scene sad, you should start out happy.

In this scene, Leslie is returning from work, so I want you to imagine that Leslie has just been praised by the boss and given a raise. Already the energy with which you enter the kitchen is different. Your mind is full of thoughts about how to spend the extra money. You are relaxed and happy about being liked and respected at work. Then you see the body.

Now you see that there is a much bigger mental shift for your character to go through. It's these mental shifts, these sudden changes in your character's thinking, that are interesting to watch. Each one of these single moments goes toward making up your entire performance.

That's how the public decide whether a performance is good, brilliant or just ordinary. They don't sit and analyse your performance, but every little moment that they don't find convincing undermines your whole performance because, subconsciously, the audience does not believe it. So finding those changes between the beginning and the end of a scene and making them believable is vital.

You ran out of the kitchen too fast

Actors do this instinctively because they think they are being true to the text and, because there is no dialogue to reveal the character's thinking, why hang around?

The actor who rushes out of the kitchen door is still hooked into stage acting, where thought is revealed through dialogue.

Screen acting is driven by thought, not dialogue. By running out of the kitchen too quickly, you miss the key moments in the scene. Revealing the character's thoughts on seeing the dead body is a real film moment. And you have to fill it with thought. So how do you do that?

How to Fill a Moment with Thought

We have to start by being very clear about what our character is thinking at each moment. Let's use the character in the last exercise as an example.

I've never found a dead body, and I hope you haven't either. But once, when I was an actor staying in very rough digs, I found a dead rat in the bathroom. I nearly jumped out of my skin. Even just remembering it I can feel my breathing speeding up, my palms starting to sweat. I immediately turned and rushed out into the hallway, virtually falling through the bathroom door in my desperation to get away from the dead rodent.

That was my instinctive reaction to something frightening and shocking. I think it would be yours too, and probably not dissimilar to your reaction to the body in the kitchen. So, as that was our very real reaction to seeing something shocking, shouldn't we do something similar on screen?

Yes, but before rushing out of the room you have to reveal and expand your experience at seeing the body on the floor. Screen acting is about playing with time and expanding moments. By expanding the moment when you see the dead body, you allow the audience to enter the experience. It's like letting them into a racing car as you drive round a corner at high speed – they too experience what your character is feeling and become involved in your dilemmas.

So what happened in the moment when I saw the rat? And how can I transfer the experience into that of seeing the dead body?

Physiologically my body had a huge surge of adrenalin. This happens to us all if we are faced with danger. Psychologists call it the 'flight or fight' reaction. We are, after all, animals; in our case very clever and highly adapted apes. The adrenalin surge is our body's way of coping. It speeds up your thinking and causes time to slow down so that you can deal with whatever the danger is. In that tiny moment before I rushed out of the door, I had time to think:

'Is it dead? It's not moving! How did it get there? I can't see any holes in the skirting board or by the bath… By the bath! I had a bath in here this morning! Was it dead then, with me in here this morning! Or did it climb out of the toilet bowl?'

In that tiny moment of time, before I tumbled out of the door, all those thoughts flooded my mind. It was a film moment in my real life. And what exactly is a 'film moment'? It's a point of high drama, where you give the impression of expanding time on screen as you reveal your inner monologue to the audience. We've all experienced these moments in real life, and how often do people who've been involved in a dramatic news story describe their experience as being 'like something out of a film'. Of course, if a terrorist is waving a gun about on a plane it's easy to imagine the terror the passengers are feeling, but not all film moments are so obvious or as easy to imagine as that. Films and television dramas are more likely to depend on the ordinary interplay between people in real life – no less crucial to the character's life as the terrorist on the plane, just a lot more subtle.

Your job, as a screen actor, is to find those moments and open them up for the audience to share.

How to Find Screen Moments

Every scene is filled with screen moments. You just have to find them. So let's take a short scenario as an example:

A boy and girl have been dating for a few months. The boy has finally plucked up the courage to tell the girl he loves her. Unknown to him, but known to the audience, the girl is having an affair with an older man. She decides to lie and tell the boy she loves him too.

In this scene there are four very clear film moments:

- The boy overcoming his fear that the girl might reject him, and courageously deciding to tell her he loves her.

- The girl's reaction to his declaration of love and her inner dilemma at having an affair with someone else.

- Her decision to lie.

- The boy's reaction to the good news that she loves him.

The job of the screen actors here is to take those moments and reveal all the thoughts held within them to the audience.

In a complete script, that little scene would be surrounded by many other events, lots of other subtext, and you would have much more to work with. But even with a brilliant script you will always have to use your imagination to ener- gise your screen work. Screenplays are not just streams of dialogue, but an interaction between action and dialogue that reveals the subtext. It's for you to use your own imagi- nation first to discover, and then to reveal, that subtext. Imagination is the engine of screen acting.

The script just says, 'Leslie sees the dead body, then runs out of the kitchen.' Of course you run out of the kitchen – so would I if I saw a dead body on the floor. But you have to make sure that you reveal your thoughts in that moment before running out of the door.

How to Reveal Your Thoughts to Camera

A good way to start is to write down the character's thoughts as an inner monologue. Each separate thought should lead naturally to the next. When you see them written down you'll immediately identify those that are extraneous or that block the flow of the scene. All the useful thoughts should lead to actions; the useless thoughts are passive. Cut them out or rewrite them if you're dissatisfied. Remember that the thoughts should flow naturally into the character's actions as written in the script.

So for the dead body exercise I might write:

> I think I'll open that bottle of champagne in the fridge and celebrate… I can't wait for my pay rise… Let's see if I can get that Porsche on hire purchase…
>
> [*I enter the kitchen.*]

What's that smell? That's odd... And what the hell is that shadow by the table?... That's not a shadow... It's a body... Shit!... Who is it?... Are they dead?... They're not breathing... I can't see their face... I can't recognise the clothing... What should I do?... I don't want to get too close... What if they have a terrible disease? A virus... Don't be ridiculous... Who the hell is it? And why are they in my kitchen! They're not moving... They're dead... Oh my goodness! What if someone killed them? The murderer might still be in the house... I can't hear anyone moving... Call the police!

[*I run out of the kitchen.*]

When you're finished you should have a complex web of thoughts on the page. Some of the thoughts will be dynamic, some will simply get in the way. Cut those out and stick to the dynamic ones. For instance, in my stream of thoughts the whole side issue that the dead body might have a virus gets in the way. Much better to go from, 'They're not breathing' to 'They're dead!'

Keep cutting the thoughts until you have a very clear narrative:

I'll think I'll celebrate... I'll open the champagne... Can't wait to get that Porsche...

[*I enter the kitchen.*]

What's that...? A body! Who is it? Are they dead? They're not breathing. They've been murdered. Where's the murderer? Are they still here? I've got to get out of here!

[*I run out of the kitchen.*]

Each thought has an action attached to it; an energy flows directly from the thought:

I think I'll celebrate.

[*My character wants to get to the fridge to get the champagne.*]

Can't wait to get that Porsche.

[*I can see myself driving the new car, see people admiring me in it.*]

[*Now I enter the kitchen.*]

What's that?

[*The adrenalin rush makes me physically cautious but I must look at the body.*]

Do I know them?

[*I have to move closer to look, but I don't want to. I want to run. Fear makes me approach the body slowly and carefully.*]

Are they dead? They're not breathing...

[*I stop moving and go very still as the next thought forms.*]

They've been murdered!

[*My heart starts to beat faster, my eyes scanning for the murder weapon. Then...*]

Where is the murderer?

[*I become alert and look back into the hallway.*]

Have they left the building or are they still here?

[*I listen, hard.*]

Can I hear them?

[*I hear a faint noise. Traffic? A pipe creaking?*]

I've got to get out of here!

[*I'm about to run to the front door, but what if the
murderer is in the hall? I'm just going to have to
run fast and be aggressive. I run to the door.*]

You see from this how each thought creates an action. That
action might not be fulfilled but could be repressed. In the
above example, the thought 'I've got to get out of here' did
not lead to the character instantly running. Another thought,
'What if the murderer is in the hall?', stopped them. In that
case, the urge to sprint was repressed, and that should man-
ifest itself in the character's body and on their face.

You'll also notice that there are no emotions attached to the
thoughts. That is because emotions are the by-products of
action. You could see the dead body and write, 'I feel sad
that this person is no longer alive.' It is a valid thought but
there's no action attached, just a feeling, and one that you
can experience as an actor but will not transmit to the
viewer in this particular context. If you knew the dead person it would be different because in that case your
emotional reaction to the dead person would be part of the
narrative thrust of the scene.

A screen actor's energy is always flowing outwards. You
always want something. But if you concentrate on what you
are feeling, you risk becoming self-indulgent and boring to
watch, because while you are having a great time feeling all
sorts of emotions, the audience is feeling nothing.

This is especially true when a scene involves emotions.
Nearly all emotion is better repressed than expressed – take
crying: it's more upsetting watching someone trying not to
cry than watching tears pour down their cheeks. All emotion is a by-product of the actions within the scene.

Now try the exercise again. I want you to learn the stream
of thoughts that you've written down as you would lines of

dialogue. It's important that you use your own thought lines: if you copy mine, the pulse of the thoughts is not coming directly from you and won't be as convincing. Nor will they excite you as an artist. For instance, you might not be stimulated by the thought of getting a Porsche, but what really excites you is buying a new flat or a pair of shoes.

One of the most common faults in screen acting is what I call 'acting of acting', where an actor has copied another actor's performance. Because it's not their own creation, the pulse of the character's thoughts is not coming from their instinctive emotional centre. The audience will sense this and stop believing in the performance.

The only sure way of getting it right is to use your own imagination to stimulate your work. That doesn't mean you shouldn't look at other actors' work and evaluate it: looking at another actor's work and taking something from it is different from simply imitating their work.

Now, using your own thought lines, do The Dead Body exercise again. Already you will begin to see a difference from your first attempt. One of the most important advances is realising that, when you have a stream of controlled thoughts, it slows you down and makes you direct your energy better within the scene. But this is only the first step towards understanding screen acting.

Summary

- Screen acting is driven by thought.
- A scene is a series of moments.
- The actor has to reveal these moments to the camera.
- Each moment is driven by thought and each thought leads to an action which may or may not be carried out.
- The character always wants something (at the beginning of the scene, Leslie wanted to celebrate. By the end of the scene he wanted to get out alive).

Common pitfalls

I worked on this exercise with one actor who exaggerated everything. Feeling cheerful on entering the kitchen, he whistled and put on a confident swagger, much like a comedy window cleaner. On seeing the body he reacted as if shocked by an electric cattle prod, then he hunkered down as if being hunted by a fleet of helicopters sweeping around the kitchen ceiling. When I pointed this out to him, he remonstrated: 'But you said don't be too small... Be happy at the start of the scene... Be shocked by the body. I was all those things!' I shook my head: 'No, you *demonstrated* all of those things.'

In film and television, every reaction has to be driven by thought, and those thoughts have to be rooted in reality. Otherwise the work will be just a series of demonstrated reactions based on what the actor has observed other actors demonstrating in similar scenarios. For the actor I just mentioned, the moment of his being afraid there might be a

murderer in the house translated into his being a heroic figure – almost a war hero. He was saying, 'I think there is a
madman on the loose but I can deal with it.'

The difference between him and a true actor is emotional
memory, imagination – and artistic taste. So how do you
acquire these things?

Emotional memory is easy – we're all constantly laying
downs tons of emotional memory which you can draw on.
Imagination is the engine of screen acting and is improved
simply by practice. *Artistic taste* is a much more complex
matter. Everyone's tastes differ when it comes to acting. Even
star actors have been known to criticise each others' choices.
Personally I don't think you can go wrong if you follow
Shakespeare's advice to the actors in *Hamlet*: 'Hold a mirror
up to nature.'

If your character behaves on screen as a real person would
in real life and has a convincing inner life, you're on the right
track. Tailor your thought line and reactions to the overall
style of the story you're telling. In a comedy, characters often
test the boundaries of believable behaviour, but I still reckon
that whistling as you enter the kitchen might be a bit crass.

The film critic Pauline Kael wrote that 'Films are a series of
moments that hang like jewels on a necklace.' As a screen
actor, your job is to bring those moments to life. No matter
how much time pressure the film crew exerts on you, you
must remain calm, centred and focused on revealing your
character's thoughts to the camera as they happen, moment
by moment, as if they were your own.

Summary

- Write down your inner monologue and learn it.

- Find the moments in the scene and expand them.

- Characters are driven by action, actions are driven by thought.

- Thought – breath – action/speak.

- The camera cannot read your mind; you have to reveal your thoughts to camera.

- The exercises and techniques in this book will help to get you through the shooting process, but ultimately it all boils down to three keywords:

  PREPARATION – CONCENTRATION – RELAXATION

We'll now go on to consider each of these in more detail.

Preparation

'Success depends upon being prepared. Without preparation there is sure to be failure.'

Confucius

In screen acting, preparation is central to success: everything else flows from it. If imagination is the engine, preparation is the fuel. If you haven't done enough prep you won't be relaxed. You'll be easily distracted by the tensions and problems of the set, and this will prevent you from concentrating on being the real person in that scene, living each moment truthfully. The more fuel in the tank, the bigger the journey you can undertake.

You'll need to do a lot of preparation, and all of it alone. So where do you start?

You start with the script. For the screen actor, the subtext of the scene and the actions of the characters carry as much importance as the dialogue. Think of each scene as an iceberg: ninety per cent of what is actually happening is going on below the surface, and it's that hidden, complex web of thoughts, desires and interactions that you have to reveal.

First, though, you have to discover it for yourself. Your preparation for the part makes you part-detective, part-psychologist, combing through the text for clues that reveal that subtext.

You'll also need to do a good deal of research, but research without imagination is like a teabag without water; dry, dull and lifeless. Access to your imagination while preparing your part is crucial – it's the engine for all your creative work on the character and the world they inhabit.

'Imagination is more important than knowledge.'

Albert Einstein

Because screen acting is driven by thought, use your imagination to transform the screenplay into a coherent series of thoughts and desires. Do that truthfully; give your characters real emotions, not false or demonstrated ones. Their reality has to be rooted in your own, and for this you have to have access to your own library of memories and be able to transform these deeply personal memories into the emotional state of your character.

Let's suppose that you have to cry. When I was an actor I would always use one particular memory, which was the death of Sophie, our much-loved family cat. Sophie had been ill for some time but was suddenly rushed off to the vet after a massive heart attack. I arrived to find her in a plastic air tent, struggling for breath. When she saw me, she put out her paw to touch my hand, as she did every night when I came home. Only she couldn't, because of the air tent. Despite her weak state, she struggled to touch my hand, gently clawing the plastic sheeting until, seeing her pathetic effort, the vet allowed me to slide my hand into the tent. She rested her paw on my hand and slowly drifted off. Even now, the very thought of this brings a change in my breathing; my throat goes dry and my eyes fill with tears. Clearly, my character won't actually be in that same situation, but it brings me into a similar emotional state. Now I use my imagination to translate that feeling of being on the verge of tears into the state my character really is in.

Remember the golden rule: always repress emotion, release it only in close-up, and only when appropriate. Seeing someone repressing tears is far more affecting than watching them flow in cascades.

Strangely, recalling the death of my mother when I was young doesn't work for me. This is probably because it's too close, too personal for me to be able to transform it into someone else's world. So you don't only need to find access to these memories, you'll need to discover which of them works for you.

The actors who can best access their memories and observations of life will have a wider range of choices to make for their character. A great actor makes interesting choices. As the great dramatist Anton Chekhov said, 'Everything I learned about human nature I learned from me.'

So, let's start with the script.

Below is an example of a film script. This is the first scene of Robert Altman's brilliant 2001 film *Gosford Park*, with its screenplay written by Julian Fellowes.

EXT. THE COUNTESS OF TRENTHAM'S HOUSE. DAY. NOVEMBER 1932.

It is a grey day. Mary Maceachran, a young Scottish lady's maid, watches a liveried chauffeur trying to start a green 1920s Daimler in front of the London house. The chauffeur, Merriman, climbs out with a crank handle, which he fits and turns.

>   MERRIMAN
>   Just start, you filthy heap
>   of scrap.

>   MARY
>   She'll hear you one of these
>   days.

>   MERRIMAN
>   I don't care if she does.

PREPARATION

> MARY
>
> Don't you just?

The motor catches and he stands. While the passenger seats are enclosed, the front, driving seat is open to the weather. Mary places a basket with a thermos glass and a sealed, tin sandwich container on the rear seat. As she does so, it begins to rain.

> BUTLER (VO)
>
> Mary? Merriman? Are you ready?

With a final check, she looks up to where a butler in a black morning coat waits.

> MARY
>
> Yes, Mr Burkett.

We can hardly hear his 'everything's ready, milady,' nor can we see the face behind the veil of the figure who hurries down the steps. This is Constance, Countess of Trentham. Muffled in furs against the cold, she hurries into the waiting vehicle.

2. EXT. COUNTRY ROAD. DAY.

Merriman drives. Mary sits silently next to him, huddling into her coat. Unlike the passenger, the servants, in the roofless front set, are exposed to the rain.

CUT.

You'll see at once that this is completely different from a play script. First, we have a short paragraph above the dialogue. It always begins with EXT or INT, meaning exterior or interior.

Next comes an indication of the location. Here, we are out-side the Countess of Trentham's house. Then we learn whether it's day or night, indicating whether the scene will be shot in daylight or dark. Day, however, might be any-where from seven in the morning to late afternoon. That's for you to discover from the text.

Next comes the action line, also known as the slug line, which describes what we are seeing. In this case it's a young lady's maid who is watching a chauffeur trying to start up a 1920s Daimler.

It's extremely important that you read the action lines thor-oughly. Lots of actors skip reading them, especially if they're used to theatre work. There the stage directions – often based on the blocking from the original production – can act as a rough guide. Many theatre directors ignore stage directions, but for the film director they are as crucial to the scene as the dialogue. In film and television the action lines are vital for understanding the story and for discovering your character's actions, so read them carefully.

The scripts will also be printed on different-coloured paper. The first draft – the one that the actors and other creatives on the production work from – is blue. Once you start shoot-ing, you'll be given rewrites and these will be on pink paper.

The major difference between the film and television scripts is that television scripts have more dialogue. By and large, television scripts are dialogue-driven, whereas films are driven more by visual image and physical action.

So, what's the first step?

Receiving the Script

Your script has just arrived in the post. First, find a quiet place and make sure that you won't be disturbed for the whole time it will take you to read through it. A complete film script should take about an hour and a half. If you are doing a TV series, you might be sent the first three episodes.

Read the script right through in one go, making sure you pay special attention to the action lines. If you keep getting up to make coffee or answer the phone you'll lose concentration, and you might miss some important detail buried within the action or the dialogue.

Reflect

Now take a notebook and write down your first impressions of your character, as well as a quick sketch of the overall story. If at this point things are not clear or you are unsure of something, read the script again.

These notes are important. Later, after you have done much more work on the character, I want you to go back to them to remind yourself of what you originally thought. Sometimes, once you've done a lot of prep on a part, you can lose touch with your first impressions. As in real life, first impressions are very important.

Rest

Now put the script down for at least a day. Even if you don't have much time to prepare for the part, try to give yourself at least a chance to sleep on it. Then read the whole thing again, and write down what you think of your character and the others.

Having had a break, you will have given your subconscious enough time to digest things. You will have got over the initial excitement of turning the pages of a new script and discovering the story for the first time. Your next reading will be more considered.

Return

Now look at your initial notes and add to them, making sure that you mark the notes clearly 'first reading' and 'second reading'. Already there will have been subtle changes: you're beginning to see yourself in the situations the story throws up and planning how you'll play the part.

Now go through the script again, this time looking only at the scenes your character is in. Break each scene down into a simple beginning, middle and end.

Plot

Simply write down what is happening in each scene. Treat each scene like a whole film, looking especially for the moment of change. Some scenes might have lots of moments of change, others only one. The major change might not be to your character but to another within that scene. The important point is that you know who is doing what and to whom, in every scene you're in.

Titles

I find it useful to give the scenes titles. So in the little scene from *Gosford Park*, the actor playing Merriman might write, 'Luckily the car started again.' The actress playing Mary might write, 'Finally everything is ready and we're off.' You can see at a glance that the titles reveal the character's attitude to the scene and to the story that's unfolding, and they also give you a good indication of the story arc. In practical terms, they're an easy way to remember what is happening in a scene when you come to shoot it. This is especially useful if you're working on a long television series, under time pressure and perhaps shooting a lot of scenes in a day. If you're shooting scenes out of sequence, a quick read of your title will remind you where you are in the story.

By the end of the prep period, you will also have added a list of useful reminders as to what you want from the scene and where your character has been.

Timeline

Position your scenes into a timeline in the story. This will take time and, of course, will mean that you'll be flicking backwards and forwards through the script to make sure you've got it right. Scene One might be in the spring of the first year and Scene Two a year later, in winter. Most films are set over a matter of weeks, and often the days are not described in any detail – the script doesn't say Scene One is on a Monday and Scene Five on a Friday. In the *Gosford Park* script, it's not clear what day they are setting off. The important thing for you to work out is which scenes are consecutive and which are separated by a period of time.

Once you have all your scenes titled and slotted into the timeline of the film, you can start working properly on the character. You now have a proper framework within which to work. Without these prior steps it's easy to miss important details. What happens to your character in the timeline is crucial in terms of character development. Because film and television are shot out of sequence, it's important that you immerse yourself in the story during this period of preparation. Not only should you understand each scene that you are in, but you also need to be familiar with scenes that you are not in, so that you know what is motivating the other characters.

Summary

- Give yourself time to read the script(s) through at one sitting.

- Make notes on what you think of your character and write down the overall story.

- Break down each scene as you would an entire film, looking at its beginning, middle, and end.

- Title each scene from your character's point of view.

- Have a second reading of the script(s) and compare your new notes with those you made earlier.

- Put your titled scene breakdowns into story order.

Discovering the Character

Now we can start to explore the character. You'll need to ask yourself some basic questions, the first of which is:

Who am I?

This is your character's relationship to the other characters. Consider the world they come from in terms of class and background; what type of education have they had; what type of work do they do? What are the attitudes of the other characters towards yours? What do they say about you?

Let's be clear about what is 'character'. After all, the very nature of drama is to reveal people and the reality of their lives. People are rarely what they seem. The devoted wife/solid teacher is secretly having an affair with a pupil (*Notes on a Scandal*). The detective who discovers that his vulnerable, frightened client is the result of an incestuous relationship with her father (*Chinatown*). The head of a Mafia family is secretly having panic attacks (*The Sopranos*).

The character a person presents to the world may be – and usually is – different from that inner person, driven by their own set of desires. Character is revealed by actions, not just by what people say. Very often, what a character says is the opposite of what they really mean or what they really want. You must concentrate on what your character does within the story, but also pay special attention to what other characters do to or say about your character.

Keep writing your notes and keep referring back to the script. Perhaps no one says anything about your character? Suppose you're playing a policeman in three scenes in a TV drama and your character is mostly reacting to the other characters. Not much to go on there, perhaps. But you do have the character's job, and very often it's the jobs that we do that define us as people. Quite often in film and television you'll have little more to go on than your character's job. So use that. How did you become a policeman? What sort of training did you have to do? How long have you been doing the job? Each of these questions has resonance.

What if the script doesn't say how long you've been doing the job? Or if it doesn't say where you were educated? This is where you have to put your detective's hat on. You've been cast in the part and let's say, for sake of argument, that you are a forty-year-old male. So if you've been a policeman since you left school (and very few policemen come from another job into policing) you will have been in the force for twenty-odd years. What effect would that have on you? Look at your actions and dialogue as the character: are they cynical? Caring? Has being a policeman brutalised their sensibilities? What price have they paid for doing the job? Are they helpful, still seeing the good in people? Or has being a policeman made them suspicious of all human behaviour? These are choices you must make from the script.

And if you are a twenty-year-old woman cast in the part, does that change things? Yes, of course it does. Younger people are more optimistic, more ambitious for their careers; still sure they can change the system. And a woman's approach to things is different from a man's. As a young woman in the police force your everyday life would be spent in a male-dominated environment. How would that impact upon your character?

The most important thing for you to discover as you work through the script is in what ways the character is like you. Many actors are confused by this. They see the job of acting as being different from their usual selves: for them, good acting is creating a character that's as far from their real self as they can get.

In the past this was probably true. Audiences delighted in the ability of actors to transform themselves into many different characters, and these actors were much sought after in the profession. In the days of repertory theatre, a good protean actor was highly valued. She or he could play a range of parts over the season. In the first week this might be a juvenile leading role, in the next an old woman or old man, and then in the last show of the season, several small parts in what was usually a Shakespeare play. The audience in the old repertory theatre loved watching the actors 'act'. However, that world has gone, and with it the need for protean actors who could play a range of parts well outside their age range and type.

These days, films, TV dramas and series are all individually cast. This has changed everything – including, interestingly enough, the way theatre is cast. Most stage plays are now individually cast. If the director wants a slightly overweight sixty-year-old to play the part, he'll get one. They won't ask the forty-something actor to put on padding and a wig to play the part – unless, that is, the character has to age from forty to sixty. If they want a sixteen-year-old girl from Leeds, they'll find one. Very rarely will you be asked to play outside your acting type or age range, but we will look at this in greater detail in a later section.

Being yourself in the part is crucial to your success. Unsuccessful actors, watching others achieve success in film and television, tend to say as a snide criticism, 'Well, they're only playing themselves.' But that's the point – you are bringing a part of yourself to the role, alive and open to the realities of the scene you're playing.

Life on Screen

I once directed a short film about soldiers recently back from the Gulf War. It focused on the effect the war had on a group of young men; how the atrocities they had witnessed and been part of affected their sensibilities when they returned to their everyday lives. Because they were ex-soldiers, there was a lot of swearing when the men were alone together, and one of the actors seemed to have a problem with this. On the face of it he said the lines extremely well, but the swearing didn't sound right. He hit the expletives too hard, gave them too much emphasis.

I took him to one side to discuss the problem, and discovered that he hated swearing in real life. He had come from a very moral, religious background and only ever swore under great duress. Consequently, when his character swore he gave the expletives the same emotional intensity that he would have used in real life.

But in the film they were ex-soldiers, who swore without even being conscious of it! I asked this actor to seek out the company of men who swore a lot, and he chose a local pub where they showed a lot of football. In this male-dominated space, fans would yell obscenities at the screen, hurling insults at players and opposition fans. Then the actor got it.

He made the swearing in his part as easy as breathing, and this was especially important because it impacted on the scenes where we saw the characters with their wives and families. In situations where swearing was frowned on because of their own social codes, the absence of expletives made the men's behaviour seem very different. Their conversation was stilted, less easy, their anger harder to dissipate.

If that particular actor had not conquered his own personal loathing of swearing, the subtle differences manifested in the scenes with the wives would never have been revealed.

We humans are a complex species. We live our lives in a complex web of needs, wants and desires, where one bit of our personality distorts another. When working on your script, you must be making constant reference to yourself, your observations and your intuitive knowledge of self. Identify those bits of your personality, class, education, background, etc., that chime with the character, and make a note of anything your character does that you are unsure of or feel uncomfortable about. Don't do what hundreds of actors do and ignore them. These are the actions and character traits you will have to tackle with your research and imagination.

It might be as easy as it was with the actor in the soldier film, or it might be much harder, but it's vital that you identify any factors that will inhibit you from becoming the character. The actor I worked with was lucky in that we had a period of rehearsal, so I could spot the problem and put it right.

Mostly you don't get that luxury. So use your preparation time wisely. Remember, it's your face on the screen.

If you have been cast in the part, the director, producers and casting directors must all think you are right for it. You must have something about you that chimes with the character, otherwise you wouldn't have been cast. Besides – and here is the fantastic thing about screen acting as opposed to the theatre – only you will ever play this part. You are creating it for the first and only time that it will live.

There may be things in your own nature, however, that might get in the way of the character you are playing: things the director can't know about you. When I cast the actor to play the young soldier, for example, I didn't know he came from such a religious background. On another film I directed, an actor had to play a lothario, constantly chasing and seducing women. He managed the chasing extremely well but his seductions seemed somewhat unbelievable. Eventually we realised that the actor was secretly gay, and while he was brilliant at the witty banter and the cheeky one-liners, when it came to finally pinning the woman to the bed he could only do what he thought the character would do. We had a private chat and I convinced him that the scenes might work better if he thought of the young women as young men. The very next day his seduction scenes became believable.

Write down a list of your character's qualities as revealed in the script. Then write a list of the qualities that you and the character have in common. Be honest: no one will see this list but you. Then list those qualities of yours that you feel will work against the character. See what matches and what clashes in your list, and note any obvious gaps. If you were asked to play Merriman in *Gosford Park* you might know nothing about the mechanics of 1920s cars, but is that really necessary to play the part?

What you need to know is what it's like to be under pressure to make something work; how it feels to be desperate to keep your job. Good research about the period will help with some of the details, but just look at each scene and ask what does your character do? How do they do it? And how like or unlike you the character is at each moment. Keep digging into the script, because most of the clues are there, especially in the action lines. To go back to the start of this section, 'Who am I?' is the first question you ask of your character, and it's one that can only be properly answered by a real examination of your own psychology and personality. By delving into your own memory bank, and with a bit of research, you can build the character up from inside yourself. The screen actor cannot afford the luxury of illusion.

Summary

- Write down what your character does. What job does your character do? Research it.

- How is the character like you?

- How is the character not like you?

- Write a list of qualities that you and the character have in common.

- Note the things you find uncomfortable, or unlike you, in the character. Deal with this imaginatively by creating scenarios that help you better understand the character.

Unearthing the Motivation

'What do I want?' is one of the key questions in screen acting, because it addresses the actions and objectives of the
character you are playing. Clear objectives are the tools that
will help you enter into the character completely, instead of
playing the part blandly or just colouring a scene with generalised emotion. So what is an objective?

It's what the character wants, needs or desires. In each scene
the character wants something, and actions are the means
by which they try to obtain their objectives. This applies to
mental strategies and dialogue as well as physical actions.

The great screenwriter Aaron Sorkin, writing on objectives,
says, 'I think mostly about intention and obstacle – somebody wants something, something standing in their way of
getting it. It doesn't matter what they want… but they've got
to want it bad. And if they can need it, that's even better.'
There are several other books that deal with objectives in
great detail. The ones by or about Stanislavsky will be especially useful.

Anyway, let's assume you are playing the chauffeur Merriman in the scene from *Gosford Park* – and ask yourself the
question: 'What do I want?'

You want to start the car. You want to start the car so you
can get going. Nothing is said about the history of the car
but from Merriman's first line – 'Just start, you filthy heap of
scrap' – we see that he is clearly not impressed by its
mechanical reliability.

Merriman's objective, then, is quite straightforward: he
wants to get going. And to do that he must start the car. That
is the clear objective of this scene but, as his first line indicates, he considerers the car a heap of scrap. It might not
start.

Every character will come up against an obstacle: that is the
nature of drama. The obstacle to Merriman's objective is the

car. Mary wants to load the Countess's picnic lunch into the car and get off to her first shoot at Gosford Park, but until the car starts neither can fulfil their objective.

Always be clear in your notes about the obstacle stopping you from reaching your objective. In this scene it's simple. In another it might be a person, a political movement, a war, being drunk or a lack of information. Just be clear.

But perhaps there's more to Merriman's objective than just starting the car. This is 1932. He's a servant. He might want the car to start quickly to please his boss, the Countess Trentham, because if he should want to change jobs and doesn't get a good reference, he'll be stuck driving this filthy heap of scrap for the next twenty years.

Actions

Merriman's objective, then, is stronger than just starting the car. It's to get moving as quickly as possible in order to please his employer. That is your overall objective in the scene, so what are your actions? The scripts reads, 'The chauffeur, Merriman, climbs out with a crank handle which he fits and turns.'

In what manner does he climb out of the car with the crank handle in his hand? With what thought? With what desire? Does he do it slowly? Deliberately? Does he scramble out, or struggle out, exhausted?

                    MERRIMAN
        Just start, you filthy heap
        of scrap.

How does he say the line? He knows that words will not start the car, so why is he saying them? He's not asking for anything unusual, just for the Daimler to start. This suggests that he has had problems in the past getting it to start. Now apply your imagination.

As there's nothing in the script about what's wrong with the car – or, indeed, its history, apart from this one line from Merriman – you have to give yourself a history with the car that will stimulate your character.

For example, you might imagine that the day before, just as you were taking Countess Trentham to an important engagement, the Daimler broke down. She blamed the breakdown on your lack of mechanical skills and was very annoyed with you, but as a servant you were in no position to argue back. You just had to take the blame, and with it the knowledge that the Countess didn't think you were up to the job. You then had to spend the rest of the day and most of the night stripping the engine down to find the fault. Finally, tired and hungry, and covered in grease and oil, you fixed the engine. Now, on the morning of this very important trip, you are confronted by the car once again.

It's important that in your imaginative work you keep the stakes high. If the car doesn't start, Merriman gets sacked. On top of that, he doesn't get a reference. The film is set in 1932, so he will become yet another man without a job in the Great Depression. Being unemployed in that period meant not being able to feed your family, pay the rent or even clothe yourself properly. So the stakes are very high and, consequently, the need to please the Countess is pressing. It's also important to make sure your imagined narrative does not contradict anything stated or suggested in the text.

Delivering the Lines

Let's go back to the beginning of our scene…

You want the car to start. You also want to get to your destination on time without breaking down, to safeguard what is left of your reputation with the Countess.

Bearing all this in mind, how do you say you first line? How do you behave? Clearly you are angry at the car. Your whole future relies on it starting. So you could just say the line angrily, but anger is a feeling, an emotion; the by-product of not being in control. If you say the line angrily you will just be generalising. It might work for the odd line, even the odd scene, but across the whole piece it becomes dull to watch, and why? Because it's not believable; it's just colouring the scene with one tone.

People in real life are much more sophisticated. Even if they are enraged, anger comes out of each person in a different way, through different actions. One person might slam the side of the car with their fist, while another might control their rage by simply tightening their lips. It depends on the character. In this script, Merriman climbs out of the car with the crank handle, which he fits and turns. The clue is in the way he does it. He doesn't slam the door, nor does he hit the side of the car with his fist. The writer has chosen Merriman's character with a purpose. He sounds like a man who can control himself. Despite what is at stake, he gets out and puts the crank handle into the shaft without any show of temperament.

So now we have a clue as to Merriman's mental state, but we still don't know how he does things. That is why you need to action your dialogue with verbs. You can spend a lot of time searching for the right verb, but it isn't time wasted. It's all helping to focus your imagination on being that character in that moment.

Your action on the first part of Merriman's line 'Just start, you filthy piece of scrap' is to plead. So you plead: 'Just start…' Then, on the rest of the line, you threaten: '…you filthy piece of scrap'. The fact that Merriman talks so intimately to the inanimate car shows how agitated he is.

So on the first line of dialogue your action is first to plead, and then to threaten. You can see at once that this is specific to the moment and because of that you know how to do it – we've all pleaded for something or threatened someone.

Once you apply actions to the scene you are doing something specific, and this will help you direct your energy properly.

You can also use actions to define what physical movement your character makes. So the verb for Merriman climbing out of the car could be 'I tackle you.' He then pushes in the starting handle and turns it. I once had to start a vintage car and I know how difficult it is. It's not until the pistons lock that the real hard work of turning the engine over begins, so the point at which I prepare to turn the handle could be described as 'I dominate you'.

Ask yourself what you do when you're desperate for something to work. Or when was the last time you were afraid that something you'd done wouldn't meet with approval? Once you have found an emotional memory of your own to match the moment in the scene – in this case Merriman's inner anxiety – add it to your thought line.

As the scene moves on, things are constantly in flux. The actions within a scene or within a character's speech can vary quite a lot and quickly. A manager trying to motivate the workforce might threaten, cajole, agitate or flatter, all within one short speech.

After Merriman's line, Mary says:

> MARY
> She'll hear you one of these
> days. (To *warn*.)

Merriman's reply is simple and succinct:

> MERRIMAN
> I don't care if she does.
> (To *defy*.)

> MARY
> Don't you just? (To *tease*.)

The motor starts and he stands.

Mary's action on 'She'll hear you one of these days' is to 'warn' Merriman that the Countess might be close. Or, equally, it could be to 'scold'. The way the actor playing Mary says the line will, of course, affect how you deliver the next line. If she is warning, then I think Merriman's action is to 'defy'. If she is scolding, then Merriman's might be to 'dismiss'.

All this, of course, depends on the relationship the two characters have with each other. Having read the entire script, I know that Merriman disappears from the film after scene six, in which we see Mary's inexperience as a lady's maid exposed, much to her embarrassment. This is where we see that Merriman has clearly behaved like this so many times before. So what is the status between the two of them? Does Merriman see himself as an authority figure and therefore feel foolish at being teased by Mary? Or are they flirting? These are questions you should answer in your prep: the decisions you make about the subtext will help your actions flow organically.

I am often asked if you should action the other character's dialogue? The answer is yes. Even though the other actor – whom you've probably never met until the day of the shoot – may eventually choose actions very different from the ones you chose, practising in this way opens up the subtext and helps you to understand what is going on beneath the surface in a way that isn't just speculation. The more you practise with objectives and actions, the better you become.

Deciding the Super-objective

Objectives, like actions, can change during a scene but they all culminate in the super-objective. This is the thing the character wants most from the overall story. A detective's overall objective in each film is to catch the murderer, but not all his objectives lead to this. The objective in his first scene might be to leave the crime scene quickly because he has to get to a family event arranged by his wife. The objective of solving the murder has met the obstacle of pleasing his wife.

Every character will have a super-objective, even Merriman, whose whole story arc only spans six scenes. Describing it in your preparation will give you a clear picture of how the writer intended your character to function within the film, and playing this clearly will position you properly in the world of the script.

Moral Choices

Do not judge your character in a moral way. Even if the actions they commit are completely against your nature you must find a way to justify them. If you moralise about a character, you will only ever see them from the outside, and describing your character in the third person is a sure sign that you are being judgemental. 'She's a bully' or 'He's a tart' are mere generalisations and will not help you play the character.

Summary

- Break down each scene into your character's objectives.

- Objectives are what the character wants. Your objectives may change in the course of the scene. Make sure they are marked clearly on your script.

- What is the obstacle to your objective?

- Remember you can only play one objective fully at one time.

- Your character tries to get what they want through *actions*.

- Their actions are always described in verbs: 'I [*something*] you.'
- The action on each line of dialogue should be described by a verb.
- Objectives and actions have to be activated by imagination.
- Ask of each scene: 'What do I want?'
- Make the question personal. Even as you write your notes on the character, you are connecting yourself psychologically to the character. Place yourself constantly in their shoes.
- Make sure that all the emotional moments are supported by real memories from your own imaginative storehouse.
- Define your character's super-objective.

So now you have a clear line of scenes set within a timeline of the story. If you're working on a television series, go as far as you can with the scripts you have. More often than not you'll be given an overall storyline that will encompass all the episodes.

Finding the Context

Every entrance is an exit from another scene. Every time you enter a scene you have come from somewhere else and from a different set of circumstances.

Let's go back to the *Gosford Park* scene and this time let's assume you are playing Mary.

Where were you before the scene started? We know from the script that you have a thermos and a tin of sandwiches.

Did you make them yourself? Had the film been set in 1952 that might have been the case, but it's 1932 so the sandwiches would certainly have been made by the cook. You probably stood in the kitchen while they were being made. What sort of kitchen was it? This is where your research comes in. Find a book or look on the internet. When you have found the right type of kitchen, fix it in your imagination. Further, see the cook cutting the bread and getting the ham from the cold store. What is your relationship to the cook? There's nothing of this in the script, so again you have to invent a relationship to help stimulate you in the part. Perhaps the cook is scornful of you because you have so little experience as a lady's maid? This idea will be useful later when some of the other maids are also scornful of your lack of experience.

So you stand in the kitchen watching the cook make the sandwiches. Improvise the scene in your head; see the old cook in your mind's eye, talking about all the real lady's maids she's worked with over the years. Imagine holding your tongue as her every breath seems to insult you. You wait patiently as she makes the tea for the thermos, but really you just want to get out and on the road. You've never been to a grand house before, and never been on a big shoot. You're excited but don't want to show it in front of the cook for fear she'll see it as another example of your inexperience. She might be able to mock you now but when you return you'll be full of stories about what Gosford Park was like. Finally, slowly and with disdain, she hands you the sandwiches. Now make your way out of the kitchen to where the car is.

But hold on – how do you know the car is there? How do you know what time to set off? It must have been fixed for some time: a big shoot at Gosford Park would take months to organise. It will have been in the diary for months, so you've had many days, if not weeks, dreaming of what it will be like and who will be there. Let us say that Countess

Trentham told you the night before that she wanted tea and sandwiches for the journey and you'd be leaving at nine. Now it's quarter-to-nine. Having got the sandwiches and the thermos, where will you wait until the clock strikes nine and your magical journey to Gosford Park can begin? In the hallway, by the big clock. Then, as the clock strikes nine, you can go straight out, put the sandwiches in the car and be on your way. You wait, listening to the tick of the clock and the noises of the house; the sound of your own shoes pacing on the marble tiles… Then, overcome by the excitement of what is to come, you can wait no longer. You run outside and stand by the car, waiting for Merriman to come and start it up.

And so on. What 'your' Mary did before the scene began might be completely different from my scenario, but by creating a world for your character to inhabit, you bring reality to every moment. Stimulating your imagination connects you to the character, and the best way to do this is to create for yourself an emotionally memorable journey of some sort.

This is what Stanislavsky called 'the score of the part', and that's exactly the way that you should look at it. Imagine you are watching a film with no underscoring, no sound effects. It would be dull and lifeless, but when the underscore and sound effects are added, the picture comes to life. In the same way you can bring your character to life by creating a memorable score that gets you from scene to scene. The best screen actors look as if they have come from somewhere and are going somewhere.

Stimulating the Imagination

In this short scene from a TV hospital drama, a surgeon is pulling off his scrubs as he walks down a corridor, talking to a nurse. Clearly he has been in the operating theatre.

PREPARATION

INT. Hospital. Day

Simon Green pulls off his scrubs as he heads toward the sluice room. Nurse Parker holding a form in her hand tries to keep up.

> GREEN
> What the hell are they up to this time? When did Sawyer decide this bit of nonsense?

> PARKER
> I don't know… But Sawyer was quite clear that everyone who's part of the operating team should fill it in.

> GREEN
> Why don't you tell that jumped-up little number-cruncher that he can stuff his form where the sun doesn't shine.

> PARKER
> Mr Green, please fill the form in… If you don't I'll miss my next train and my son will have to spend another hour with his grandmother who is already fed up looking after him… Please, Mr Green, for me.

Green takes the form out of Parker's hand.

> GREEN
> For you, my dear.

The subtext of this scene is that Green, a senior but ageing surgeon, recently missed a promotion and is very bitter about the hospital's administration, especially Sawyer who, he thinks, stopped him getting the job.

So how do you bring the scene alive?

The answer is being able to activate your imagination and memory properly: it's in the thousand tiny details that you cannot write in your notes.

I want you to imagine you're in an operating theatre for an hour, performing a standard procedure. To do that properly, you need to find out what Green specialises in. Once you know that, go onto the internet and discover exactly what that operation involves. So far, so simple. The skill lies in bringing that research into the reality of your character.

If I were working with you playing Green, I would create an improvisation that recreated the concentration and tension of an operating theatre and the pressure a surgeon is under. Obviously you can't operate on anyone but you can create the right mental stimulus. I'd get a face mask, something that restricted your breathing just as a surgeon's mask does. I'd also make you wear a hat and some sort of gown – again to create the sensation of being wrapped up and hot. Then I'd give you a task to complete under a strict time limit – doing a difficult jigsaw puzzle while reciting the seven times table, for example, would stretch you in every way.

Then I would plunge you into the scene. The change in your mental energy and your stress level would be noticeable at once. The improvisation gave you a taste of the reality that the surgeon faces every day, and your imagination puts that experience into the playing of the part.

Life on Screen

I shot a film about six women trapped down a deep pothole. To give them the right feeling of claustrophobia, I put them in a dark room and had them move through the legs of twenty chairs laid out in a winding pattern. They had torches but could see very little. I had someone else in the room silently changing the pattern of the chairs. After about twenty minutes, the novelty wore off and the sheer hard work of crawling around between the chairs kicked in. The women were getting tired and thirsty. I had arranged with the group leader that she should simulate a panic attack, and on the prearranged signal she went into action. The others, not realising that this was planned, had to react in character. Within moments they were screaming at each other as the line of command broke down and another member of the group had to take charge.

After the exercise we ran through the scenes in the film where the women discovered they were trapped in the pothole. It was amazing how different they were. Already the claustrophobia and panic had fed into their performances. This was important when we shot the film because, although we were filming down a real pothole, the safety restrictions were such that for much of the time the actors were confined to a crevice at the side of a cave, pretending to be trapped.

Remember that the camera lies. Although the audience saw the women trapped in a tight space by falling rock, they were in fact just pressed into a smooth groove in the rockface and the falling stones were made of polystyrene...

But thanks to the exercise, they were able to draw on the emotional response that that imagined reality had stimulated. It was the actors who supplied the reality of the scene.

Try these exercises for yourself. If you're playing the surgeon you could easily replicate my improvisation with the gloves, mask and jigsaw. I realise that the caving exercise would be difficult if you were alone at home, but you could still place yourself in claustrophobic situations. Find a dark place where you can experience disorientation similar to that of being down in a cave. Use your imagination to bring your improvisations to life. Only you really know what will work for you. What stimulates you?

In the hospital scene, a crude or lazy actor would rely on ripping off the scrubs to reveal their anger. After all, it's just another television drama. Who really cares?

Well, you should, because excellence sells. This is incredibly important to your future as a screen actor so I'll say it again: Excellence sells.

Switch on the TV any night of the week and you will see a lot of all-right or good-ish acting. That is, the actor looks right for the part, says the lines in the right order and sounds perfectly natural as they say them. But that's all. The problem is the actor's attitude. They've fallen into the trap of seeing themselves as just another technician, and while there is certainly a lot of craft and technique involved in screen acting, if it isn't informed by the imagination of an artist, the work will remain dull and lifeless.

If you want to excel, the bulk of the work is in your prep. Do the research, put in the effort, and it will show.

And it shows most in the edit. When the director is on the floor of the set or location, he or she has a thousand problems to solve. Very often, once they've got the moment in the scene, they move on. But it's in the cool and calm of the edit that the director really sees how consistent an actor has been and how good their work is.

Excellence will always be recognised – and remembered.

Summary

- Do improvisations that stimulate your imagination to illuminate the character's direct experience.

- Write down the journey that the character has undertaken to get to each scene.

- Research should feed directly into the character. Don't just gather general stuff.

- Go to places that stimulate your research (e.g. country houses for *Gosford Park*). Anywhere that will give your imagination something concrete to work with.

- Have a view on what clothes your character would be wearing.

Choosing Your Costume

When doing your preparation, think very hard about what your character is wearing. One of the first things you will be asked about when you do a TV series or a film is what costume you think might be right for the part. Young actors are usually surprised at this, but it's a key question. Once you have the script fixed in your mind, research the manners and habits of the period to see what your character might wear.

The first creative you meet after the casting director and the director will be the costume designer. Sometimes they'll take you to a costumiers for a fitting or, in a modern piece, they'll take you out shopping. If you haven't thought it through, you could find yourself wearing the wrong clothes and this will affect your performance.

Summary

- Read the script straight through without interruption.
- Write down your first thoughts about your character and how he or she interacts with other characters.
- Leave the script alone for a couple of days, or at least overnight, to give your subconscious time to start work on the part.
- Write the story of the script down. This will make sure that you have understood the structure properly.
- Analyse the scenes you are in, breaking them down into beginning, middle and end, as if they were little films in their own right.
- Title the scenes.
- Note where and what changes happen to your character and to the others.
- Place the scenes into a timeline for the film.

Who am I?

- Write down your relationship with the other characters.
- Character is revealed by action: what are your character's actions?
- What do the other characters say about your character? What do you say about yourself?
- What do the other characters do to you, both physically and mentally?
- What job does your character do?

- Write a list of qualities that that character has. Then list the ones that you have in common with the character.

- Which bits of your personality will get in the way of being the character?

- Remember you have been cast in the part. You and only you will ever play the part.

What Do I Want?

- Break each scene down into your character's objectives.

- What obstacles stand in the way of your achieving them?

- How your character tries to get what they want is with their actions.

- Actions are always described by verbs: 'I am *doing something* to you.'

- Set out your objectives and actions in every scene clearly.

- Everything is driven by your character's super-objective.

Where Have I Come From?

- Improvise to stimulate your imagination and illuminate the character's experience.

- Write down the journey that your character has taken to get to each of your scenes.

- Research about the world of the character should feed directly into the character in the script. Not

> just a general understanding of period or historic
> setting,
>
> - Go to places that will stimulate your imagination.
>   Places that will bring the script alive for you.

This might seem like a lot of work, especially if you're only
playing a small part. But please believe me when I say that if
you do the work, it will bring you results. You will present a
character with real depth. An actor who has done little or
no preparation will not be able to make bold choices on the
day for fear of revealing that they don't really know what's
going on. They will make errors of detail in the character,
tempted to play cliché instead of reality. They'll have little or
no contact with the subtext of the scenes, and no understanding of how their part functions in the overall drama.

Once you have a firm grip on the story and your character's
place within it, you can begin to play. That's the great thing
about giving yourself a good foundation: it gives you room
to manoeuvre and develop the character when it comes to
shooting.

The unprepared actor is stiff and unreactive compared to
the actor who has done their prep.

Life on Screen

*I directed an actor who had, I could tell, done little
work on the part other than learn the lines, and this
became abundantly clear when I gave her a note on
one line within a speech. I felt the whole intellectual
attack on the speech to be too slow. It was plodding,
when actually the character had a mind like a steel
trap and the other characters should have felt*

> *intimidated by her. For the next few takes after I gave her the note, the actress kept forgetting her lines and eventually I had to let her go back to her plodding delivery just so I could complete the scene on time.*
>
> *Because she had done hardly any prep, she only had the one way of doing it.*
>
> *It's a small industry and word of mouth travels fast. Actors who prove themselves good, reliable and flexible get more work. Sadly, the opposite is also true.*

Exercise: Preparing *Gosford Park*

Here are two scenes from *Gosford Park*. Choose a role, then go through the script implementing all the aspects of preparation we have discussed in this section.

- Mary Maceachran, a young maid to Countess Trentham.
- Mrs Wilson, could be any age over forty, housekeeper of Gosford Park.
- Barnes, forty-something, valet to Lt. Commander Meredith.
- Merriman, fifty-something, chauffeur to Countess Trentham.
- Elsie, twenty-something, thirty at a push, head housemaid.
- Robert Parks, early thirties, valet to Lord Stockbridge.
- Mrs Croft, sixty-something, cook at Gosford Park.
- Henry Denton, a young valet to Morris Weissman, a guest at the shoot.

To make the exercise work you should follow all the steps in the preparation section. Of course you will not always be the perfect age or type for the part. The important thing is that you start to understand the process.

Clearly you won't be able to do all the necessary research or create improvisations that would open up the character's experience, but just sketch out ideas to show how you'd pursue these. There's no right or wrong in this work: it's just about looking hard at the text and imagining it in your mind's eye.

INT. KITCHEN CORRIDOR. DAY.

Chaos reigns. Servants duck past the piled-up trunks and cases. Valets and maids (Barnes and Sarah, joined later by Renee and Robert) struggle to check that none of their luggage has gone to the wrong rooms. Surveying it all, clipboard in hand, is Mrs Wilson, the housekeeper, an opaque woman in her middle years. Barnes, who is carrying a large, flat, crested case, approaches. Mrs Wilson does not look up.

> MRS WILSON
> Just leave everything in one
> pile, make sure it's
> properly labelled and it'll
> be taken up.

> BARNES
> These are the *guns*. Where's
> the gun room?

His voice could scarcely be more disdainful. She nods at a side corridor.

> MRS WILSON
> At the end on the left.
> You'll find the keeper, Mr
> Strutt, in there. He'll show
> you what to do.

PREPARATION

> BARNES
> I know what to do.

He goes as Mary arrives timidly,
sheltering behind a laden Merriman.

> MRS WILSON
> Yes?

> MARY
> Hello.

> MERRIMAN
> The Countess of Trentham.

Merriman has carried in the three smart
cases. He knows the ropes. Mrs Wilson nods
and checks her list, handing a label to
the man.

> MRS WILSON
> Leave them over there by the
> luggage lift and tie this to
> the top one. You'll find the
> chauffeur, Mr Raikes, in the
> courtyard. He'll tell you
> where to put the car. You'll
> sleep in the stable block
> with the grooms.

He sets about the task, leaving Mary
feeling more alone than ever.

> MRS WILSON (CONT'D)
> Her ladyship is in the Blue
> Damask Room. You'll be
> sharing with the head
> parlourmaid. She'll show you
> where everything is. Elsie,
> this is Miss Trentham.

A young, uniformed maid, Elsie turns at
the sound of her name and comes near.

[60]

                    MARY
        Excuse me, m'm, but… my
        name's Maceachran…

                    ELSIE
        Not here it's not.

Mrs Wilson has moved away as Elsie takes
Mary's case.

                    MARY
        What about the jewels?

She indicates the dressing case still in
her hand.

                    ELSIE
        This way. George is in
        charge of the safe. He's the
        first footman. And you want
        to watch where he puts his
        hands…

They turn another corner in the maze of
service corridors that run beneath the
house. At the door of the butler's silver
pantry stands a supercilious figure in
livery. Next to him, just inside the room,
is a large wall safe. The iron door is
open revealing a felt-lined closet, filled
with laden shelves. George, the first
footman, is receiving a case from another
maid (Renee). Mary takes a key on a chain
around her neck under her dress and opens
the case, removing the jewel box, which
she is about to hand over.

                ELSIE(CONT'D)
        Have you got the ones for
        tonight?

                    MARY
        Oh…

PREPARATION

Mary unlocks the box. Inside are gleaming
trays, each one with a complete parure of
gems. She takes out a set of sapphires and
puts them in the pocket of her coat.

> ELSIE
> Always take a separate box
> with the first night's
> jewels. Saves bother.

Mary nods, relocking the box and handing
it over to George, who gives her a wink as
he takes it. As they walk away, recrossing
the back hall, they almost collide with a
tall stranger carrying a suitcase. Mrs
Wilson arrives.

> MRS WILSON
> Elsie, this is Lord
> Stockbridge's valet. Show
> him the footmen's staircase,
> will you? And he'll need the
> ironing room.

She starts to leave. The new arrival turns
to the two maids.

> ROBERT
> The name's Robert. Robert
> Parks.

This seems to halt the retreating Mrs
Wilson. Robert looks at her enquiringly.

> MRS WILSON
> I meant to say you'll be
> sharing with Mr Weissman's
> man. You could have gone up
> together but I don't know
> where he's got to.

Other business claims her. Elsie sighs.
They might as well get on with it.

PREPARATION

> ELSIE
>
> Has his lordship's luggage
> gone up?

> ROBERT
>
> Supposedly. He's in the
> Tapestry Room, wherever that
> is… Oh well, here we go
> again.

But Mary cannot return his casual
pleasantry. Instead she half-whispers.

> MARY
>
> That's just it. I've never
> done a house party before.
> Not properly…

> ROBERT
>
> You'll be all right.

Elsie, above them on the back stair, has
overheard.

> ELSIE
>
> How d'you manage to be taken
> on as a countess's lady's
> maid if you didn't 'ave no
> experience?

> MARY
>
> She wants to train me. She
> said she didn't care about
> experience.

> ELSIE
>
> She didn't want to pay for
> it you mean.

INT. KITCHEN. DAY.

A handsome face displays the brilliant
smile of Henry Denton, Morris Weissman's
valet. At the long table, the cook, Mrs
Croft, is working on a tray of quail. The
senior kitchen maid, Bertha, slices
carrots and the junior, Ellen, slowly
turns an ice-cream churn. They ogle the
visitor who speaks in a Scottish accent.

> MRS CROFT
> Get on with your work. Yes?

> HENRY
> I just —

But before he can say more, Mrs Wilson
spies him from the corridor and enters.

> MRS WILSON
> Ah, Mr Weissman, there you
> are.

> MRS CROFT
> I'm dealing with this. What
> is it, Mr Weissman?

The dislike between the two women is
almost tangible.

> HENRY
> Well, to start with my name
> is Denton. Henry Denton.

> MRS WILSON
> You are here as valet to Mr
> Weissman. That means you
> will be known, below stairs,
> as Mr Weissman for the
> duration of your stay.
> You'll find we keep the old
> customs. It avoids
> confusion.

He would answer back but decides against it.

> HENRY
> It's about Mr Weissman's diet –

> MRS WILSON AND MRS CROFT
> Yes.

> HENRY
> He's a vegetarian.

> MRS CROFT
> A what?

> HENRY
> A vegetarian. He doesn't eat meat. He eats fish but not meat.

> MRS CROFT
> Well, I never.

> HENRY
> I'm sorry if it's inconvenient.

> MRS CROFT
> Well, it's not very convenient, I must say. Doesn't eat meat? He's come for a shooting party and he doesn't eat meat?

> HENRY
> Mr Weissman doesn't intend to shoot. I think he just wants to walk out with them. Get a bit of air.

> MRS CROFT
> *Get a bit of air?*

> MRS WILSON
> Thank you. We'll make the
> necessary adjustments. Now,
> if you'd like to get one of
> the servants to take you
> upstairs… Mr Weissman is in
> the Mulgrave Room and you'll
> be sharing with Lord
> Stockbridge's valet.

Henry nods his thanks and walks out of the
room, watched by Mrs Croft.

> MRS CROFT
> He's very full of himself, I
> must say. Doesn't eat meat!

> MRS WILSON
> Come along, Mrs Croft. We
> don't want to be thought
> unsophisticated, do we? Mr
> Weissman is an American. They
> do things differently there.

She goes, leaving Mrs Croft seething.

> MRS CROFT
> I'll give her
> 'unsophisticated'!

Her assistants giggle but their response
does not please the cook.

> MRS CROFT (CONT'D)
> What are you gawping at?
> Those are no good. I said
> 'julienne'. And, Ellen, that
> is ice cream you are
> churning, not concrete. Calm
> down.

CUT.

The main points of the exercise are:

- Break down each scene into its beginning, middle and end.

- Mark all the points of change, not only for your character but also for all the others.

- Be clear what your character wants at the beginning of the scene and how they try to get it.

- How do your objectives change through a scene?

- Where has your character come from?

- Identify the aspects of the character that you need to research.

- Begin to have ideas for improvisations that will help you understand the character better.

- Write lists of the qualities that you and the character share.

- How are you different from the character?

- What is it about you that could get in the way of playing the part?

Now when you walk onto the set you know that the hard work is done. This is the moment to let your character interact with the other characters. In many ways it will come as a relief to be working with the other actors, but remember that you have to be able to adapt.

If you were playing Merriman, you'll have had a certain 'Mary' in your mind's eye, but the Mary you work with on set will almost certainly be better than the one in your imagination, because she is real. React to her as a real character and she will respond likewise. Now, put the preparation for this scene to one side – you have to trust yourself now.

I realise that some of what I say might seem contradictory. I talk about the amount of preparation you have to do, then tell you to 'trust yourself' and just 'run with the ball'. But this isn't really contradictory. The best analogy is that of the racing driver. He can study the track for months, practise for hours but, come the race, he must trust that everything has been absorbed into his subconscious. In the actual race you can't imagine the track as you did when you were practising. The circumstances have changed. Other drivers crowd the track; your best driving line is blocked: you have to be intuitive and adapt to the reality of the situation. Without preparation the driver may well crash because at the crucial moment, when he needs to know the exact camber of the road, the angle of the corner, his precise braking point, he will fail. Without the prep he won't be able to function instinctively at the highest level. So it is with the screen actor. Unless you've done a lot of prep, you simply won't be able to fly.

Because screen acting is driven by thought, there's also contradiction attached to another word I use a lot in this book: thinking.

Many of the exercises ask you to break everything down into thought lines, actions and objectives. That is to help you understand that screen acting is as reliant on your visible reactions as it is on the vocal tone and stress you place on a line of dialogue. Slow your thinking down so the camera can read it. Isolate your thoughts so that you only have one at a time. The audience needs time to understand what your character is thinking, to watch you shift between thoughts. But I will also say (and here is what seems to be a contradiction) that you must react within a scene unthinkingly – or instinctively, and in character. Just trust that having done the prep – having understood what the character wants, learned the subtext of the scenes, understood that action and reaction are as important as dialogue – you will be the character.

Screen acting is both difficult and easy. Once you have confidence in yourself, your talent and your choices, you will begin to realise that it is easy. But if you take your eye off the ball, lose concentration, stop doing your preparation or become complacent, the skill you have developed will desert you. In many ways, screen acting is rather like being an athlete. You train for years and years, ready to be in the moment for one brief period of time. Like an athlete always pushing to go faster, higher, the screen actor is reaching to be more truthful, more real, more in the moment. And like the athlete, you spend ninety per cent of your time working alone. It can be tough, lonely and exhausting. But do the prep and keep your mind focused on the prize, and you'll make it.

As Benjamin Franklin had it: 'By failing to prepare, you are preparing to fail.'

Concentration

Improving Your Concentration

Being totally concentrated focuses your mind and allows you to enter the world of the character completely. Your daily worries or personal problems no longer inhibit you from fully inhabiting the character. It's rather like entering the zone that top athletes talk about when they compete: being absolutely in the moment, now. And that takes enormous concentration.

It's important for the screen actor to understand what sort of concentration is needed on a film set. I've seen any number of diligent actors work extremely hard at concentrating, but all they do is create tension in their bodies so that their acting becomes strained. To understand concentration properly, you need to know a little about brainwaves, because our brains operate on different frequencies depending on what we are doing.

- *Delta waves*: These occur when we are in a deep, dreamless sleep.

- *Theta waves*: These are present in those moments between dreaming and waking, or when we are awake but just letting our minds drift. Daydreaming. These waves are great for creative and inventive thinking.

- *Alpha waves*: These waves appear in our brains when we are relaxed and creative. They're very common in children when they are playing.

- *Beta waves*: These are busy, dominant brainwaves.

They appear when we are being competitive or need to win an argument, or when we are under stress.

Unfortunately, the attitude of many actors to the word 'concentration' is a hangover from their school days. They associate concentration with the state in which they took exams, or tests – or even auditions. This is completely the wrong state of mind. The concentration you need to practise is the kind you enjoyed as a child when you were playing. Think back; try to recapture the memory of yourself as a child and the ease with which you entered your own fantasy world, where an empty cardboard box could become a space ship and then in the next moment the counter of a shop. That's the state of mind for screen acting – put bluntly, it should be child's play. That shouldn't be misinterpreted as a childish state of mind, but as that easy condition where your imaginary world just appears around you.

To do this you have to enter what the great acting teacher and director Stanislavsky called the 'circle of concentration'. Other acting coaches call it your 'bubble of concentration', but whichever, it's how you cut out all the nonsense on a TV or film set that can interrupt your concentration. You need to develop the ability to think about one thing for a long period of time. We're all used to our fast-paced lives, with phones constantly ringing, endless channels on the television, the internet and emails, but this whole host of distractions means that these days people rarely concentrate on any one thing for any length of time.

So how to start? We will do a lot of concentration exercises but the root of them all is your basic mindset.

You must be positive. Negative thoughts break into your circle of concentration more quickly than anything else. Say you've just done a quick run-through of a scene and are standing waiting to discuss it with the director. At that moment he's discussing a possible shot with the Director of Photography. You feel vulnerable. You've waited a long time to do the scene and now, having done it, you are getting no feedback. Nothing positive is being said. It's at that moment that the doubts begin to creep into your mind. For me they're like the long trailing weeds at the bottom of a lake. As the motorboat stands idling, the weeds start to wrap themselves around the propeller, and by the time you're ready to go again, the propeller is completely clogged. This is what happens to your confidence if you allow your concentration to be invaded by doubts.

To help you develop your powers of concentration, we'll start with some simple exercises. You have to do them regularly to improve.

Exercise: Mercury

Find a private space and make sure that you won't be disturbed for at least an hour. Now sit on a chair, don't cross your legs, and place your hands in your lap, palm upwards. Close your eyes, take a deep breath and hold it for five seconds. Now exhale. Do it again. Then again.

Stare down at one of your palms and now, as you take a breath, curl your fingertips upwards into a fist. Breathe out and release your fingers, opening them like the petals of a flower in perfect time with your breathing. Breathe in, closing the fingers of your hand again as your lungs fill with air. Now breathe out again slowly.

Do this for at least a dozen breaths, making sure that your fingers open and close in exact timing with your breathing.

Now imagine that you have a tiny blob of mercury on the tip of your forefinger. Mercury is incredibly slippery stuff, very reactive to movement – if you move too quickly, the blob will just slide off your finger.

Your task is to keep the tiny blob of mercury balanced on the tip of your finger as you start to close it up into a fist.

Don't make a full fist this time, just bring your fingers together, keeping the blob of mercury at rest on the tip of your forefinger. Then let it run all the way down your finger as you unfurl.

Stay relaxed, and don't forget to breathe. Slow and easy. Focus your entire mind on that tiny blob on the end of your fingertip.

It takes time to perfect this exercise. At first you do it too easily, in which case you are not imagining the mercury correctly. Sometimes it takes twenty or so goes before you really start to see it on your fingertip.

Once you've mastered the blob of mercury on one hand, I want you to try it on the forefinger of your other hand. Most people start the exercise with their writing hand, as this is their dominant hand. The other hand might prove harder, but just keep focused.

This is just one of several simple concentration exercises that I would like you to do every day. Just as a pianist has to practise chords every day, and the violin virtuoso practises scales, actors must hone their concentration.

Once you've mastered this particular exercise, ten minutes should be enough to get you going.

Focusing Your Memory

Screen acting is all about memory in action, and memory is closely tied to concentration. The next exercise pulls together your memory and concentration in a way that will focus your mind.

Exercise: News

Record part of a news broadcast from the television – five minutes, no more. Now I want you to watch it, bearing in mind that I'm going to ask you questions about the content. You'll have thirty seconds to answer these, so have a timer handy.

NB: Do not read on until you've watched what you've recorded!

Okay, now you've watched your news broadcast, set your stopwatch or get someone to time thirty seconds for you, and then answer these questions:

- What was the lead item on the news?

- What was the first picture or image you saw?

- What was the newsreader wearing (or both, if there were two)? Description and colours, please.

Now watch the recording again. How did you do?

Most people will say something like: 'Er, it was a story about banking… The first picture was money, I think.' But very few remember what the newsreaders were wearing. It's amazing how little we really take in. Or is it? Neuroscientists and people who study how our brains take in information are nearly unanimous in their belief that we actually take in virtually everything we see and hear. It's just our mental filing systems and the way we retrieve the information that vary. And pressure distorts the way your mind works. If I had given you five minutes, it would have been much easier.

It's useful for you to know this, as it will help with your character analysis. We retain information about the things we enjoy, what we feel comfortable with. For example, many people struggle with maths at school. However, I know a football fan who reckons he is functionally innumerate but can tell you by what margin his team beat so-and-so ten years ago, how many points they had any time in the season – he'll even tell you who got substituted. As the season ends, he'll be full of mathematical possibilities as how many points teams will get from the outcomes of up to a dozen games. He loves the game, and part of that love is absorbing all the details. He's probably not even aware that they are statistics.

Another friend knows everything there is to know about sailing boats. He will tell you in all seriousness that he is stupid because he failed a few exams at school, but when you point out that he regularly uses trigonometry to find his location at sea, he'll shrug and say that's simple. It's simple for him, because he loves sailing and is constantly needing to find his location. The fact that it's trigonometry is a by-product of that love.

As the great philosopher Aristotle maintained: 'Everything I have learnt, I have learnt sideways.'

So we know that everything goes into our brains, but how much detail we remember depends on how much we need to know the information. Watching your news broadcast, you knew you'd have to remember something from it, but in everyday life that isn't often the case. As an actor you have to develop your memory, and that is dependant on your degree of concentration.

Exercise: News II

Now I want you to watch and record another news pro-gramme, this time all the way through, and then I will ask you another set of questions.

NB: Again, please don't read on until you've watched the programme.

Now you have a minute to answer the following four ques-tions, so get your timer ready.

- Describe the newsreader's hair – colour, style, length. If there are two, describe both.

- What was the top news story?

- What was the first line the newsreader said?
- Describe the first filmed news clip – the subject matter and what you saw in the footage.

How did you do? Better this time, perhaps, but still missing stuff and probably not anywhere close to getting it done in under a minute. Never fear; this is just an illustration of what we all miss. What we have to do now is hone your concentration so that such exercises become easy.

A lot of books about screen acting seem to shy away from the business of developing concentration, but without concentration and memory, the screen actor will flounder.

Sharpening Your Senses

The five human senses process all the information that we receive. Each of the primary senses has a different role to play in how we perceive the world and how we remember what happens in it.

Smell

Smell is one of our most evocative senses. A waft of a certain smell and we are back in the school playground when we were twelve. Once a smell activates a memory, it is profound: the whole memory is revealed, like a complete dinosaur fossil being exposed after being hidden for millennia. It's almost impossible to remember a smell, but when it hits us it instantly brings back that precise moment, the very place where we first smelt it.

I'd like you to go on a short journey, one which takes you to places with vivid smells. Food markets, perfume halls, museums, art galleries, paint shops – anywhere with a distinctive smell.

When you are standing in one of these places, try to remember what that smell reminds you of. You'll be surprised at how many things come to mind. Take a notepad and write them down. It might just be a flash, an image; it might even be something disturbing, but try to concentrate your mind on that memory.

Do this in as many different places as you can, and write down as much detail as possible. By the end of an afternoon your head will be swimming with memories. The next part of the job is to hold on to them.

Go home with your notebook and start your concentration exercise. Sit on a chair. Once you are fully relaxed and concentrated, focus your mind back to the memories evoked by the smells during the day. See how much more detail you can remember.

By doing this exercise you are cultivating your memory storehouse, activating routes in your mind that you travel in years to come. The more you do this exercise, the more easily you'll be able to access your memory store.

Sound

Collect as many varied pieces of music as you can, preferably evocative music from every era of your life so far: music you first danced to, kissed to, did your homework to. Make sure you are in a relaxed state of mind and start listening. Let the memories come, and very soon they will be flooding in. Write them down, capturing as much detail as possible: who was doing what to whom, what was going on, what was the subtext of that moment? Try to remember the inconsequential stuff, like what you were wearing, even what you were thinking at the time.

Keep listening, concentrating your mind on remembering those memories. Each time you evoke a memory, you will get better at retrieving it from your store; bringing it back to life, so to speak. But it isn't enough just to get a momentary flash; this exercise demands total concentration in order to retrieve the memory in all its tantalising detail. After just a few attempts, you'll find your powers of concentration increasing dramatically.

In art, nothing is wasted. Eventually you'll be able to use all these memories in your screen work.

Touch

This exercise is not only great for preparation, it will also develop your concentration. Personally, I find that holding an object gives me a greater sense of the scene's reality. The way we handle everyday things reveals a lot about our state of mind.

It's a freezing cold day; you've been out in it for hours and for the last forty minutes it has been raining sleet. You come home and make yourself a hot drink. I want you to imagine the way you handle the mug. Immediately you see in your mind's eye how you cup the mug in both hands to get the warmth. You lower your face over the steam rising from the mug, enjoying the heat. With that memory, your body reacts automatically, relaxing just as we all do when we get warm after being cold. The touch of a cold marble slab can work in the same way.

Life on Screen

I recently visited a writer who lived in a small farm-house cottage. We were talking about her work and I noticed that as she talked about the early years with her late husband, she would gently run her hand across the top of the large wooden kitchen table. It was a small movement, barely noticeable but, curious, I asked how long she'd had the kitchen table.

> *'It was the first gift my husband ever bought me,' she said. 'And it was on this table that I first started to write.' Unconsciously, she was reminding herself of that period as she spoke.*
>
> *At first the marriage had been happy, and the table held such delicate fond memories of that period for her, so she unconsciously stroked it. But then, she told me, the relationship eventually broke down, and at this point her hand withdrew from the table. It was a small thing but very revealing of both character and memory.*

Things have memories attached to them. Give yourself another day trip, this time specifically based on touching and holding things. Junk shops and bric-a-brac sales are good destinations for this. The second half of the exercise can be done simply through continuous observation of the real people in your life. Watch how people touch and handle objects. Observe how people's work affects the way they touch things – a butcher's hands, for example, handle things very differently from those of a librarian. It's surprising what you discover from these observations. As Carl Jung observed, 'Often the hands will solve a mystery that the intellect has struggled with in vain.'

Remember, none of these 'sense' exercises will work if your concentration is scattered. Every time you do one, commit yourself to it completely.

Sight

We are visual creatures; our memory is largely made up of images. We remember in pictures, and one of the easiest ways to learn is through pictures. As a screen actor, you just have to retrain the way you see. As we discovered with the news-broadcast exercise, we spend too much time looking without remembering. We see, but let it just wash through our minds. Proper looking involves concentration: without that you won't remember.

There are two major problems with looking. The modern world is constantly competing for our attention and to get it, advertisers, newspapers and television channels bombard us with visual images. The result is that, overloaded and spoilt by a surfeit of fantastic imagery, we have stopped looking properly.

The other problem with the way we look at things is the Protestant work ethic. We are not encouraged to stand and stare. We must be achieving, doing things, creating things… The idea of 'just looking' doesn't seem to fit the modern mindset, and if you do it, you're made to feel guilty. It begins in childhood: 'Don't just sit there staring into space, do something!' 'What are you looking at?' someone will shout if you stare in his or her direction. The consequence is that we have stopped looking properly. As the tramp-poet W. H. Davies had it, 'What is this life if, full of care, we have no time to stand and stare.'

The life of the screen actor should be full of time to stand and stare – that's how you gather your raw material.

So how do you look properly? You concentrate on the detail.

Life on Screen

I once visited the National Portrait Gallery in London with an artist. She took me round and talked about pictures I'd seen hundreds of times, but the way she looked at these pictures was quite different. She saw the detail. I would walk up to the same picture, admire it and move on. But I hadn't really looked: I'd given the picture a glance, been touched by the sur-face sensation it gave me, and moved on. But by studying the picture in detail for a long time,

> *analysing its every part, then standing back and tak-ing in the whole again, my artist friend opened the door to a new way of looking.*

Once you allow yourself to concentrate on the detail, you begin to discover in the pictures all sorts of things that you've never seen before. The key to retraining the way you see is fighting off any initial boredom and concentrating properly. All these exercises make you focus your mind and help you get over the modern need for constant stimulus to keep your attention. Glory in the minutiae of detail, and when you think you've got everything from the object you are looking at, look again.

Exercise: Observation

Take a trip to your local art gallery. Select five pictures or sculptures to study and give yourself at least ten minutes in front of each one. Now analyse the details, ignoring the gremlin on your shoulder, attempting to distract you and telling you to move on. Because sight is the most promis-cuous of our senses, it really is the most difficult to focus. We take the way we look at things for granted. Every day we see things that are filled with history and meaning, but we just pass them by. We've seen that, and we move on. But have we really looked? And, crucially for you as an actor, this applies equally to people. Marlon Brando, one of the world's best screen actors, was once asked why he so much hated being famous and he replied, 'It stops me from doing what I need most for my work.'

'What's that?'

'Watching,' he answered, 'it stops me watching people.'

Just stand in the street for five minutes and watch people. Really look – see how they move, what they wear, how they interact with others. Where are they going? What do they want? A screen actor's source material is all around you, all the time. Watch people's eyes: where do they look, how often do they look at each other? Look at their hands. What story are they telling, what are they hiding? And don't let yourself be distracted by the worries of the day as you do this: when you are looking, you are working. It's a guilt-free excuse to stand and stare.

The three great pillars of screen acting – preparation, concentration and relaxation – are all joined together. You cannot do your preparation properly unless you are in contact with your memories and your own sensations. Without concentration they will just be a jumble of sensations. Without relaxation your concentration will be shallow and easily interrupted.

Exercise: Observation II

Actors often ask how they can keep their talents and skills honed whilst they're not working. This can be a big problem, as nobody works continually and you can very quickly find yourself getting stale. But whatever you are doing, you'll be meeting real people in the real world, and the basic clay of your craft is observing real people. Try to understand what motivates them; what drives them, what disappoints them. How do they manage the full complexity of their lives? This exercise is a version of Julia Cameron's 'Morning Pages' exercise from her inspirational book *The Artist's Way*. I've found it very good for keeping memory and concentration focused when you're not acting.

At the end of a working day, give yourself ten minutes – longer if you can spare the time – to write about what you've seen. Point out to yourself what was interesting, what was odd. Who's driving who mad at work, and why?

Describe the people. What is motivating them? How are their inner lives affecting the way they interact with others? How do they dress? Do their clothes reflect the inner person or are they trying to conform, trying to be someone else? Again, the devil is in the detail.

This exercise works well when you concentrate your full attention on it. I remember one actor becoming resentful about it, treating the notes as if they were homework. I pointed out that they would make him a better artist; he just thought they were a waste of time. He wanted to do 'proper acting'. Needless to say, that actor has since dropped from public view. But let his attitude be a warning to you. Concentration and memory need to be worked on. You don't magically develop them because you get a big part in a television series.

Keep working on your concentration and memory exercises. They will ensure that, when the moment comes, you'll be ready and able to concentrate for twelve hours a day.

Relaxation

Relaxation is one of the most misunderstood aspects of the screen actor's skills. Many people think it's just lying on the sofa watching TV, or sitting back in a comfy chair, but that isn't a state of relaxation, it's collapse – and it certainly isn't the type of relaxation you should be aiming at.

The relaxation needed for screen acting is an absence of stress in the body and the muscles, and an absence of fear from the mind. For most actors, nerves are a big problem. They always have been and always will be. Actors need a lot of courage and confidence to do what they do. It takes a lot of nerve to stand relaxed on a film set, where everything seems almost designed to create tension. You're left for many hours alone with your doubts and then you have to do a scene with relative strangers, becoming a real, living human in whatever scenario the writer has come up with. Then you just get started when you have to stop again, for the lights to reset, for someone's make-up to be checked or the camera team to practise the dolly movement. Everyone's needs seem more important than the actor's. And even the tiniest bit of tension will show.

Screen actors through the decades have coped with the stress in different ways. Marilyn Monroe was so terrified that she couldn't sleep, which meant that she was constantly late, adding even more stress. One producer who worked with her on her last (sadly unfinished) film, *Something's Got to Give*, witnessed Marilyn being violently sick before stepping onto the sound stage. For over a decade Laurence Olivier would beg his fellow actors not to look him in the eye during a scene because it would unnerve him. And the great actor-director Orson Wells would drink two or three glasses of port before going on set for a challenging scene.

A word of warning before we move on: It's important to learn how to relax properly, rather than going down the self-medicating route. A number of actors have ended up alcoholics because they took the odd drink on the morning of the shoot, to 'take the edge off their nerves'. Very soon this became a habit, until they were unable to function without drink. The same is true of pills; beta blockers and a whole range of other medication can help with relaxation, but they're not the answer.

It's crucial that you discover the true way to relax in a stressful environment. Being relaxed will give you the energy that will go into your part. True relaxation will enable you to explore the part emotionally. That is why, in the section on preparation, I barely mentioned the emotional state of the character. Emotions are the by-products of action (and the actions of other characters on you), but you will not be free to release them if you are tense. Instead you'll be forcing them out of yourself, and that simply doesn't work on screen. Once you become emotionally clenched, you are forced to demonstrate the emotion rather than to feel it and release it naturally.

And how do you achieve this perfect relaxed state? It starts, as does so much else, with your breathing. Just thinking about something stressful makes you tense, and tension makes you breathe more rapidly. Your muscles, especially ones around the face and throat most necessary to the actor, start to tighten.

So, first you need to centre your breathing. That means that you are breathing right into the core of yourself, not taking little shallow breaths at the top of your lungs.

Exercise: Meditation

Find a quiet spot where you won't be disturbed. Lie on your back on the floor, making sure that you place something under your head. A thick book usually does the trick, but don't use a pillow as this will be too soft and will distort your neck muscles. Obviously, if you have a medical condition this would aggravate, don't do it or seek medical advice first.

Lift your knees so that your legs make an arch with the floor. Make sure that this feels natural and comfortable, then place your hands on your middle, just below the ribcage. For the moment, do nothing. It's important to remember that doing nothing – being in a neutral physical and mental state – is very important to relaxation, so find your neutral state.

Now let your body spread out across the floor. Don't flop your arms and legs out but imagine that your muscles are turning to jelly and your body is spreading out. Let go of your tensions and congratulate yourself as you feel your muscles unlock – this is a huge achievement.

Now take three deep breaths, making sure that you hold each one for no longer than five seconds. Feel the breath spreading into your body and swirling around your lungs. Now imagine that gravity is pulling you down into the floor. Do not resist; let it pull you right into the floor.

Next, imagine that you are lying in your safe place. Even better if you've had to go on a journey to this place, as this gives texture to your imagination and makes it more real. Everyone's safe place is different. Mine is approached through a small country churchyard on a bright summer's day. The sky I see through the trees is clear blue and dotted with clouds. I hear birdsong; a blackbird singing to mark its territory. I enter the church through an arched doorway. It is cool within, and lit by the glorious sunshine dappling through stained-glass windows. I walk up the nave towards the altar. There is a door to the side of the aisle; a thick wooden door with wide iron hinges and bolts. It squeals as I open it. I enter a small stairwell that twists down into the crypt. There is a little light from a small doorway opposite me. I walk to this door, open it and find a small chamber with a bed, a table and a lamp. I shut and lock the door and lie on the bed, knowing that I am completely safe. Nothing and no one can get me here. I allow myself to be completely relaxed as I lie on the bed within the room.

That is my safe place. Yours could be under some palm trees on a beautiful white-sand beach. Or in the tower of a castle. The captain's cabin on a submarine. Wherever it is, it should make you completely relaxed.

Once you're in that state of mind, imagine yourself walking into an office to meet with a director about a big television series. Imagine first waiting outside the office. Try to make it as real as you can. Imagine the furniture, what pictures might be hanging on the wall. People the corridor with other actors waiting; all of them a lot like you. And then hear your name called. You enter the office and meet the director and casting director; they smile at you. You sit, and in the moment you do this I want you to imagine that you are at your brightest, smartest and wittiest. The director thinks you're great. The casting director smiles, clearly impressed. They give you some pages of the script to read. You glance at it and immediately the story is clear. As you read it through, you spot the moment of change and instantly know what actions you'd like to play. The character objectives are clear and simple. They ask you to read the script, with them reading in the other parts. Even as you read you can feel the director being thrilled by your performance. With every second of this brilliant interview that passes through your brain you become more relaxed, more present. The director asks you to read the script again, this time giving you a couple of helpful notes. You know exactly what the director wants. The second reading is even better than the first. The director thanks you for coming, and says, 'We'll let you know soon.' And you leave the interview knowing that you gave your best. You couldn't have been better.

Now gently bring yourself back to your conscious state. Don't just open your eyes and leap up, but do it gently, letting the happiness from your imaginings remain in your mind like an afterglow.

I want you to repeat the relaxation exercise every day, except each time you are in your place of safety, vary what you imagine. For example, what makes you nervous – meeting people at parties, perhaps? Then imagine you are going to a party; people it with folk you would like to impress, people who may be useful for your career. At the party you are funny and relaxed, your stories are listened to with fascination and people seem to be falling over themselves to tell you theirs. You listen, knowing that everyone in the room adores you. Yes, adores you; not just liking, but adoration. Believe me when I tell you that this simple exercise will change how you approach these particular situations.

Remember the last interview you did. Were you tense? Yes, you probably were because you wanted the job, wanted the people interviewing you to like you and want you to work with them. Because we have never been taught how to deal properly with our mental states, our minds usually fill with negative thoughts at this point. We can't prevent memories of the times we have failed from crowding into our minds. The primitive part of your brain wants to run and hide, but your logical brain knows that you can't. You have to deal with all that excess adrenalin being pumped out by your endocrine system, preparing your body to run. Before you know it, you're sweating and hyperventilating. To deal with this, your logical mind becomes a strict parent to what it sees as its frightened self, 'Now pull yourself together! How pathetic are you, getting into a state over an interview!' It's this ridiculous inner-doubt system that the relaxation exercise will deal with for you. You only have to believe in it and do it regularly, and it will work.

Positive thoughts have to be driven into your subconscious like nails into wood. Most of us are programmed completely wrongly. Subconsciously we expect to fail, so despite all our best efforts to succeed we are sabotaged by our doubts and fears. But if we turn our inner consciousness around and focus our imagination on the positive things happening to us – especially in those circumstances where we are usually nervous – our subconscious can easily be reprogrammed for success. And a major part of that success is being relaxed. Being relaxed will mean that you'll be present in the scene, as well as present on the set.

I've seen many a nervous actor subconsciously wishing they weren't on the set, sometimes so much so that they seem to shrink. They'll do anything to please the director, just so that they can finish and get away. They take no pleasure from their work, which is of course small and cautious, and the effort makes them look unnatural and forced. Tension creeps into the voice, which tightens and loses its flexibility. No longer are they being the character in the scene, they're just trying not to look nervous on set. Soon, directors won't want to work with these actors because their work is small, nondescript and fearful. And all this because the actor, while eager to please, lacks the ability to relax and do their best. Even a hint of tension can inhibit a great performance. The way to prevent tension spoiling your work is to learn to be relaxed and open to the situation.

Stanislavsky said, 'At times of stress it is especially necessary to achieve a complete freeing of the muscles.' Don't think of this exercise as a little sideline to the real job of acting: it's crucial to your success. Do it every day, especially coming up to an interview or a job, and you'll see the results.

Tips for Relaxation

There are some practical classes that might help with relaxation. Also, being with other people and having a regular class to go to will make sure that you are constantly improving your ability to relax properly.

Meditation

This is useful for centring the mind and body with your breathing.

Alexander technique

Frederick Alexander was an Australian actor who kept losing his voice on stage. He analysed his physical moves when acting and discovered that tension made him push his chin out as he spoke, putting great strain on his vocal cords and consequently leading to him losing his voice. This encouraged him to look at the whole physical shape of the actor, and how bad habits could inhibit proper relaxation. He developed a method that enabled the actor to direct just the right amount of energy to every action, including speaking, and to make sure that it was properly focused. Classes can be expensive but after five or six you will begin to understand the tension in your body and be able to apply what you have learnt in class to your work at home.

Hypnosis and self-hypnosis

These can be effective methods of reprogramming your mind away from the negative tensions that inhibit your work. Some people are suspicious of hypnosis because of the popular image of the stage hypnotist who persuades someone to behave like a chicken when a trigger word is used. The serious business of hypnosis, however, is completely different from such carnival sideshows. Firstly, you could never make yourself do anything you didn't want to do, so the idea of a hypnotist secretly controlling you is nonsense. Secondly, it works only if you want it to work. Many of the exercises in this section are intended to stimulate a state of mind in which you can start to alter your programmed responses to stress and fear. A hypnotist is just someone who can help you through the process. But a note of caution: it is a field filled with charlatans, so track down a good hypnotist and check their references. If they're good at what they do, they will offer you at least three satisfied customers. If they can't, or you don't like the look of them, move to another.

T'ai chi

This branch of Chinese martial arts is an excellent discipline for exercise, balance and centring your body, whilst freeing your mind from the clutter of day-to-day worries.

PART TWO

Practice

Film-making

To understand screen acting properly we must first under-stand the process of single-camera film-making and appreciate the actor's role within it. I now want to look at the way single-camera film and television is made, including a breakdown of key crew members, and how a simple scene would actually be shot.

It's important that you understand the mechanics of shoot-ing. Most actors can imagine being someone else, but achieving this in the technical medium of film is a different matter. An actor who understands the mechanical process of film-making will be able to focus their energy properly in order to sustain their performance right through a scene and ultimately through an entire drama. Filming is first and fore-most a mechanical process. It brings into being the world created by the screenwriter. This is then focused artistically by the director's imagination. The role of the screen actor is to turn the character into a living, breathing human being who fulfils his or her dramatic function. All this within the timescale and the financial pressures of modern film-making.

A dinner-party scene involving six characters may take an entire day to shoot. The actors may have to start the party in high spirits and end it in drunken anger. Each actor will have to chart the considerable emotional shifts through the scene in great detail. Sustaining a performance over the whole day, while the scene is constantly being broken up into different sections, takes both concentration and detailed preparation. Not knowing the mechanics of shooting has been the downfall of many fine actors who, after exhausting themselves in the first seven or eight slates, find that when it comes to their close-up at the end of the day, they have nothing left to give.

Life on Screen

I once shot a film about a drug rehabilitation group. At the end of the film the enthusiastic young drug counsellor, who started out with so many great ideas, sits alone in a church hall, weeping at her failure. She has realised that her ineptitude has destroyed the group. I shot a series of wide angles of her sitting alone in the circle of empty chairs, weeping. Then, moving in for her close-up, I found that her tears had formed a small puddle around her feet – she was quite literally sitting in a pool of tears. So when it came to her close-up, she had no tears left. Simply because she didn't understand the process, she had cried herself dry. Not understanding the mechanics of shooting, she hadn't saved her tears for the close-up.

Summary

- Film and television are mechanical processes: you have to understand the rhythm of the set.

- Save your best for your close-up, while still being real and generous towards your fellow actors.

- Be friendly to the crew: they want a professional actor, not a new friend.

- Fear can make actors behave in a pompous and arrogant manner. Stay open and relaxed, right from your arrival on set.

So let's begin with the professionals who will be filming you...

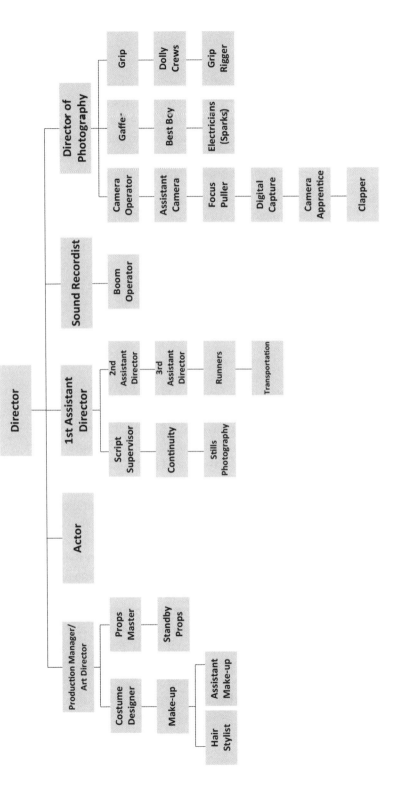

The Crew

The film crew has a strict hierarchy (see the diagram on the previous page), which is essential to know if you're going to understand what is going on. Actors who don't know what is happening around them often get in the way of important crew members, and this makes them appear amateurish and unprofessional.

So, let's go through the crew members and what they do, and how best to work with them. Remember that I'm outlining who works and what happens on a professional film set – but if you're working on a low-budget or student film, it's certain that someone will be doing each of these roles, even if they're called by a different job title or sharing the responsibilities differently.

Director

The most important person on a film set is the director. The director has already worked with the writers to bring the script to life, and they have worked with the producers on the overall production values of the film. The same is true in television. They will have agreed principal casting, as well as the film's shooting schedule.

Please remember that, while the director is up at the top of this pyramid, there is also an inverted pyramid above them – made up of producers, executive producers, sales companies and distributors – who will all bring pressure to bear on the director about what they see coming from the film set. Actors are rarely sacked; directors, sadly, are, and mostly for not being able to get 'a performance' from the actors. Please remember that the director has chosen you and cast you in this role, so help them to make it work. There will also be many other voices on set whispering about how badly a director is at their job – but never get involved in gossip. It is so easy on a film set to lose contact with the director, so make sure you keep working creatively with them, as an artist, to create a believable and compelling character.

A director may have been attached to the project for months, sometimes even years. They will have worked with all the various heads of departments on how the film will look and how it is to be shot, within the financial constraints set by the producers. The director carries a vision of the film in his or her head. However – and this is important for the actor to know – while they may be fantastic film-makers, they might not be good with actors. I know this seems strange but many directors come from the technical side of film-making, where their knowledge of actors and acting is gained just by watching them do it. They sometimes have little grasp of the actual process of acting.

On a television series all of the above will still be true, but with the added complication that the series will be directed by a whole group of different directors. So you might have one director for episodes one and two, followed by another for episodes three and four. In this case the directors are even more dependent on the actors to monitor and produce consistent performances across the episodes they're in. In many cases, the actor will get no acting notes at all, just help with blocking and emotional temperature. You have been employed to bring the character to life. The director's job is to tell the story with the help of your character. Here are some tips about how to work with directors.

- *Never question the director*

  Never question why the director is doing a shot in a certain way. There may be many reasons of which you are not aware. Your job is to make the character believable within the scene being shot, and within the style set by the director. Do not think you are being useful by suggesting a quick way a scene could be shot, or that there's a better position for the camera.

- *Always listen to the director*

  And listen carefully, because in the pressured environment of a film set, it's easy to miss a vital piece of information. I have often given an actor a note, only to realise during the next take that they have completely forgotten or totally ignored it, and usually this is because they haven't listened properly.

  There are other people involved in the shooting process, too, who might give you the odd note. The director of photography (DoP) might ask you to lean slightly forward on a particular line, so that the light can hit your eye at a certain angle. Standby props might ask you to handle a prop in a certain way. Listen carefully, and you'll be able to follow the simple hints they give you. But if you don't, you might misinterpret the DoP's request and lean forward for the entire scene. The director will not appreciate that.

  A good tip is to repeat back to the person what they have said to you. This helps you remember and prevents simple misunderstandings.

- *Be sensitive to what the director wants*

  Directors are creative people in their own right who need to know that the people they're working with are prepared to be flexible. The director, alone out there on the set, needs your help and support. Be sensitive to their needs. Come forward with ideas about the scene if you like, but don't swamp the director. If you sense a director is unsure about what you're doing, give them the chance to tell you in their own way and their own time. The director has cast you in the part; they want you as that character, so help them achieve this.

  You have to bring your performance to the set ready to be moulded. You may have to use all your intuition and insight to work out what the director wants – but that is part of your skill.

Listen to the director and try to interpret what it is they want. Your skill lies in translating what might be just a visual or verbal clue into a whole character on screen.

Director of Photography

The DoP helps the director choose the right lens for the shot, and lights the entire scene. Their primary concern is the 'look' of the film.

It's important that you, as an actor, respect and assist the DoP. Often they will ask an actor to cheat (lean) themselves to the left or the right, or perhaps lean back into a light. They are doing this so that you will look better. Any actor who refuses, thinking that leaning to the left will interfere with their performance, has no business being on a film set! Screen acting is a technical medium: if you can't be seen, the shot won't work. If the shot doesn't look good, the director won't use it. The actor's job is to make the slight move work. Simple as that.

First Assistant Director

The 1st AD is in charge of the set. In a television studio, this role is covered by the floor manager, outside there may be an AD as well. They organise the crew in setting up the shot and make sure that everything runs smoothly and safely.

The 1st AD liaises with all the other departments, heading off problems and alerting heads of department as to what's coming up next, so they know what to get ready. The 1st AD runs the set, directs the background action and works with the extras. They are a bit like the ringmaster of a circus, coordinating everything that happens on the set. In fact, if you were watching the filming from the sidelines, you might well take the 1st AD for the director. They will have already worked closely with the director on scheduling the film in pre-production, and will have a good grasp of the director's vision. The 1st AD has two assistants.

Second Assistant Director

The 2nd AD is mainly responsible for the actors, going between the set and the trailers or dressing rooms. Their job is to take actors to wardrobe and make-up, and then bring them onto set. As an actor, the 2nd AD is your main point of contact.

Third Assistant Director

Working with the 1st and 2nd ADs, the 3rd AD manages the perimeter of the set, keeping non-essential persons out of the way.

Below them are the runners, who are there to field for the ADs – and very often literally have to run and fetch things. You should remember to treat everyone with respect – my first job on a film set was as a runner.

Boom Operator and Sound Recordist (Head of Sound)

As you would expect, they are in charge of sound. Most of the sound on the film will be recorded from a microphone on the end of a boom pole, but sometimes actors will also be radio-mic'd. Radio mics are tiny microphones attached to the actors' clothing. The boom operator does just that, holding the microphone as close to the actor's mouth as possible without being seen in shot. The sound recordist mixes the various tracks as the scene is shot.

From the actor's point of view, the boom operator is important because at the start of each shot they will dip the microphone into shot to find the top edge of the frame, and this will help you to see the size of the frame.

Gaffer

This is the person in charge of the lights and the power supply. They tell the sparks (electricians) what lights are needed and where they should go. The 'Best Boy' (who can, of course, be either gender) is the gaffer's foreperson.

Grip

The grip is in charge of everything that might be needed to move the camera, such as dollies, jib-arms, Steadicams, and metal track.

The Process

Once you've gone through the scene with the other actors, been to make-up and wardrobe, and the scene has been lit, you will finally start shooting. The procedure leading up to the moment you start being filmed is the same the world over and it's the rhythm of film-making, so it's crucial that you understand it from the start.

Before each take, the 1st AD will call for quiet on set (in a television studio, it's the floor manager who does this). That means that all departments involved in the filming must now be quiet and focus on the scene.

The 1st AD will call 'First positions', the signal for the camera, sound and actors to move to their starting positions for the scene.

The 1st AD will then call 'Standby'. This means that everyone around the set and all the crew involved in the shot must be ready to go.

The 1st AD then will call for 'Final checks'. This is where hair and make-up move in to check your hair and make-up are correct for the scene. (When you do your filming exercises you can skip this bit, as you won't have hair and make-up ready to run into your kitchen.)

Then the 1st AD will call 'Turnover', which means the camera and sound systems should start rolling. Although digital these days and nothing actually 'rolls', the terms are still used.

When the film in the camera has reached shooting speed (twenty-four frames per second), the DoP calls 'Speed'. Even in the digital age there is a lag between pushing the 'go' button and the camera actually recording.

The sound recordist will then call 'Sound rolling', to indicate that the sound system is up and running.

Next, the 1st AD will call 'Mark it' – the instruction to the clapperboard operator to 'mark' the shot by writing the scene and take numbers onto the clapperboard. This is then placed in front of the camera at its point of focus. The scene and take numbers are called out and the two sticks marked with diagonal stripes at the top of the clapperboard are snapped together, making a crisp click. This marking means the sound and vision can be joined together in perfect sync later on in the edit.

Once the clapperboard operator has moved out of shot and the 1st AD sees that the actors and crew are ready, they will call 'Action'. Some directors like to do this themselves but most let the 1st AD do it so that they themselves can focus on their monitor and the actor's performance. Some DoPs may also say 'Set' before the 1st AD calls 'Action', to indicate that they are ready.

At the end of shooting the director will call 'Cut'. This tells the camera to stop shooting, sound to stop recording and the actors to stop acting. The director is the only person who can call 'Cut', although in rare circumstances – for example, where a crew member or actor is seen to be in danger – the 1st AD will step in and make the call.

Never come out of character or break your concentration until you hear the director say 'Cut'. Directors often let the scene go on beyond its natural end in order to see if something interesting happens. Sometimes an actor is so immersed in the scene that they do something real, unrehearsed and completely spontaneous, and on screen that can be absolutely electric.

Exercise: Taking the Take

You must learn to wait for the 1st AD to call 'Action'. The tension on a film set can be such that it's easy for an inexperienced actor, eager to please, to go too quickly, starting to speak and move before they hear the call, speaking their first line just as the clapperboard is being taken out of the frame, or the moment they hear the word 'Action'. Starting a scene too soon not only makes an actor feel foolish but has bad repercussions as often it means that the scene is cut.

So practise this simple exercise. Your character has to come through a door with a sheet of paper in their hand and say to another character off-camera:

'You'll never believe it! I've just inherited a million pounds.'

Couldn't be simpler. Now set your camera phone up and get your operator to focus on you in your end position. That is the spot where you say your line after opening the door. Mark the spot where you are standing with a piece of tape: this is your mark. (More about marks on p. XXX.) When you come round the door you have to stop on your mark. Say the line as if the person you are speaking to were just a few inches to the right of the camera. This will give you your eyeline. Either get someone to stand there or mark where you need to look with a piece of tape. You say your line to that actor or to that mark.

Now to start the exercise, go to your starting position behind the closed door. On a film or television set this is called your first position. After you have done a take, the 1st AD will call, 'First positions', and crew and actors then return to their starting positions. For this exercise, your first position is behind the door.

Get your camera operator to call out:

'Standby.'

'Turnover.'

They will then start their camera and call 'Speed', followed by:

'Sound rolling.'

'Mark it.'

If you can find another friend to operate a 'clapperboard' that would be useful – just a sheet of paper with the scene and take number written on it will do. The important thing is that they call out the scene and take numbers.

Then finally, 'Action!'

You then rush through the door with the great news that you are a millionaire.

Now, ask yourself some basic questions. Where has your character come from? What is their state of mind? Yesterday they could have been told they had a life-threatening illness, or that they have lost their job. Or they could have just split up from the love of their life, in which case the inheritance has a certain irony to it. Those decisions are yours to make, but you must make them. Any line said without the context of your character's state of mind or what they want will be meaningless and, consequently, boring to watch.

The thrust of this exercise, however, is to get you to remember the tempo of the build-up to shooting. Do the exercise at least ten times until you can remember these words in your sleep: 'Standby... Turnover... Speed... Sound rolling... Mark it... and Action!'

Whether or not you have a camera, it's also good to write down the sequence several times. Constant repetition drives it into the mind, so that when you are standing on a real film set and feeling nervous, you won't forget the rhythm.

As we go through the upcoming exercises, you should repeat the shooting routine on every exercise you film.

Technical Skills

Having covered the procedure up to the moment of filming, we will now look at the way scenes are actually shot.

This is the stuff that all good film and television actors take for granted but everyone who wants to work in the industry needs to know.

- Single-camera shooting
- Continuity
- Eyelines
- Frame size
- Dialogue
- Hitting your marks – including stepping onto a mark; swaying or shuffling into shot; turning into shot; sitting into shot; standing up into shot.

A lot of books on screen acting separate out the technical things you need to know as if they were simple tricks. For me, however, the techniques that you need for acting on screen are intrinsic to the way that you build your perform-ance, allowing you to develop and control your character within that technical medium. It's up to you to reveal the character's thoughts and make them into a living, breathing human being. If your continuity is all over the place or you don't know how to hold and expand a moment, your screen career could be a short one. For me, what is often described as 'the technical stuff' is as essential to building a character as understanding the subtext of the dialogue or knowing your objectives and actions. Sit into shot in the close-up more quickly than you did in the wide, fail to react, or to be consistent in the emotional reality of the scene between different slates, and you could lose valuable screen time.

But if you can, try to:

Find each moment of the scene afresh each time you do it. Be able to match the emotional temperature and physical movement between slates. Stay alive, open, vulnerable and free whilst the machine of the film crew grinds around you. Hit your marks. Manage to shift your eyeline to a piece of tape on a lump of polystyrene and still be truthful. Then you're on the way to success.

So let's break down these technical skills.

Single-camera Shooting

Some television programmes, mostly soap operas, are still shot 'multi-camera'. This means that several cameras are placed on the set in fixed positions and record the scene simultaneously from different angles. This gives an impression similar to live theatre and is often used for filming in front of a live audience but – as it demands a large sound-stage and a fixed set, and is consequently very expensive – it's used less frequently these days. A lot of contemporary soaps also shoot on a regular outdoor 'set' – Albert Square in *EastEnders*, for example, or Coronation Street itself.

All film, and most serious TV dramas and serials, are shot with a single camera. That means that a single mobile camera covers every angle in a scene. If there is a lot of movement within the scene, the director will sometimes use a Steadicam to cover the action. A Steadicam is a lightweight rig attached to the operator's body, with a camera fixed to a robotic arm. This balances out the body movements of the operator as they walk along, ensuring that the camera can move smoothly around and in front of the action. You see a lot of Steadicam shots in TV series like *The West Wing* and *ER*, where actors are talking and walking through multiple locations, in and around a lot of extras. Operating a Steadicam is a highly skilled job, and the machine and its operator are usually hired in by the company for use in particular scenes.

We will now look at how a standard scene would be shot using a single camera. Read the following and try to imagine how the scene might be shot.

INT. KITCHEN. DAY.

Julia sits at the kitchen table looking down at an empty coffee cup. Her fingers fiddle nervously with her wedding ring. The front door opens and Nathan, her husband, walks into the kitchen.

She does not look round.

> JULIA
> I'm sorry, Nathan. It's not…
> (She stops talking.) Anyway
> I've made up my mind. I've
> decided… I'm leaving.

She gets up, passes Nathan and enters the hallway. Picks up her suitcase and heads to the front door.

> NATHAN
> You said you'd stick by me…

Julia opens the front door.

Nathan goes to the kitchen table and picks up Julia's wedding ring.

Julia closes the front door behind her.

CUT.

The scene is taken from a drama in which a man, in this case Nathan's father, has been discovered to be a serial rapist twenty years after his crimes were committed. The film is about what happens to the rest of the family as they absorb and react to this knowledge.

Just six short lines, but there's a lot going on beneath the surface. Remember that, for the screen actor, the subtext is crucial. Film scripts are like icebergs: ninety per cent of the information about the world of the character is beneath the surface of the text. Your job is to be part-detective, part-psychologist, hunting down the clues that reveal the character and their inner thought processes.

When you arrive at the location you will have a run-through of the scene. The 1st AD and the DoP will also be present, along with the director. The director will probably start by telling the actor playing Julia where to sit, and then you'll run through the scene. This is a loose, almost casual rehearsal, but do not be fooled: many key decisions are being made. Sometimes the director has a very clear idea how the scene is going to be shot and they'll tell you where to stand, what to do at any given moment. Another director will follow the pulse of the actor, asking them just to do whatever they feel with the scene.

How can you tell the difference between these different styles of directing? By being open and listening.

If the actor playing Nathan instinctively moves across the kitchen and sits opposite Julia, the director might stop the run-through and ask him to stand at the back of the kitchen and play the scene from there. This is because it looks better on camera. Why? Because the camera loves depth. It would also be a strong indication that the director has a clear vision of what they want in the scene.

Often in film and television you are placed in what seem like odd positions in relation to the other characters. Again, this is because it looks better on camera. You might be asked to 'cheat to the left a bit' or 'cheat in a bit' to make the shot work better on screen.

Do not turn to the director and say 'In the reverse I was standing like this!' The director and their team will be aware of this. A reverse is the shot that mirrors the current one – if it was over your shoulder, the 'reverse' will be over the other actor's shoulder.

Now we'll look at how the scene will actually be shot.

The director will decide how many set-ups are needed to cover all the action; let's say, thirteen set-ups or slates. On a television film I would probably do the scene in fewer slates. Television is shot much more quickly than film but it still needs the actor to be supplying the same degree of truthfulness.

The slate is the clapperboard, on which is written all the information that the editor will need to know in order to edit the sequence. The clapperboard is placed in front of the camera before every take. It notes first the title of the film, then the director's name, the name of the DoP and the date, but the key information is the scene number, the slate number and the take number.

So this is Scene 27 in a film called *Somebody's Father* and let's say this is the first scene that we will shoot in the film. So it will be marked up:

Scene 27 is quite simply the twenty-seventh scene in the film.

Slate 1 means that it is the first set-up in the film.

Every time the lens on the camera is changed or the camera is moved, the slate number is changed, the numbers increasing.

A single drama may have between 250 and 900 slates, depending on the budget. The more slates, the more coverage and the greater the options for the director when it comes to editing the film.

Take 1 is the first take. Most directors will have negotiated a ratio of how many takes they do per slate with the film's producers. The average is a ratio of 1 to 6, which means the director will do a minimum of six takes. They may do more, they might even do less, but six will be the average for the film.

Sometimes the scene might be being shot on two or three cameras at the same time, which means you might be working on two or three slates. It might be 'cross-shot', which is when a camera is recording the action over each actor's shoulder, or when there is a lot of action and the director wants to capture it from different angles.

Now I'll describe how the scene from *Somebody's Father* will be shot with one camera in the standard way.

The first set-up, or slate, is a wide shot of Julia sitting in the kitchen.

Slate 1 covers all the action, right up to Julia picking up her bag and leaving, although from this wide angle Julia's leaving and Nathan's reaction to it won't actually be seen. The director will still cover all the action, just in case it's needed later.

This is a good angle for the actor playing Julia to reveal to the camera her anguish over her decision to leave Nathan, while not disclosing that anguish to Nathan.

You should note where the camera is placed in relation to you and the other characters, so you can see where and when you can best reveal your inner thoughts. We'll look at this in greater detail later.

The director will shoot a number of takes until they are satisfied that they've got the shot. That means they are happy with the performances and the way the shot looks on camera.

Once the director has done the wide shot, whatever you've done in the scene is fixed in stone. This is why it is essential that you make the right choices in your preparation. If, when you come to your close-up, you think to yourself: I should have stood up there instead of here, it's too late.

The decision is made. If you made a passive or an unconvincing choice, that's tough – you're stuck with it, while the director shoots all the other slates.

The next slate is a medium shot favouring Julia.

We see Nathan over Julia's right shoulder. Again, the director will let the action run all the way to the end of the scene, and the actors get to reveal their thinking when not being observed by the other character. This allows you to switch between your character's private thoughts and the face they present to the other character.

The next shot is a close-up of Julia.

This slate will run only until Julia stands up and wipes frame (meaning the camera stays still and the actor walks out of the frame).

In a close-up you get the chance to reveal all the character's inner thoughts to camera, just as a soliloquy in the theatre enables the character to talk directly to the audience.

The next slate is a close-up of Nathan facing Julia.

Again, this slate will run until Nathan wipes frame as he walks to the kitchen table to pick up the discarded wedding ring. From this angle we will not see Nathan's face as he says his line as Julia leaves the kitchen, but we will see it before and after her leaving. This gives the actor playing Nathan the chance to reveal his thoughts before she leaves, and all the pain after she has gone.

The next slate is Nathan watching Julia going to the front door. This is where Nathan says, 'You said you would stand by me.'

An inexperienced screen actor would probably have put all their preparation into this line. Those with experience will see the line coming out of a series of thoughts and actions. This one is just verbalised.

This slate will run until Nathan sits at the table.

The next slate is Julia looking round at her husband and saying, 'I've decided… I'm leaving.'

Note that the close-up of Julia saying the line 'I'm leaving' is shot only after she has been filmed leaving Nathan several times, so the true emotion and thought that drives the line, along with her knowledge of what it will do to her husband, have to be sustained over many shots before she gets to say it in close-up.

The next slate is a tracking shot of Julia leaving. This means that the camera will move on a dolly – a sort of wheeled cart – beside Julia as she gets up and walks to the kitchen door.

And then the slate (tracking shot) continues following Nathan back to the table.

The next slate is the close-up of Nathan with the ring.

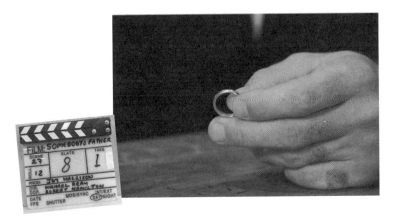

The next slate is Julia with the ring.

The next slate is Julia picking up her bag and heading through the front door, hesitating on the step before leaving.

The next slate is Nathan coming back from work and spotting the bag in the hallway.

The actor playing Nathan, therefore, has to do the beginning of the scene after he has done the main section of his wife leaving him.

The next slate is the close-up of Julia in the doorway.

The close-up is done after the two wider shots because the lens has to be changed. So, again, the actor has to sustain credibility from the wide shot into the close-up which is shot later.

The next slate is Nathan's point of view (PoV) of Julia's suitcase as he enters.

That, then, is the series of slates that will cover the scene. The director will probably do six takes of each, plus cutaways – shots of inanimate objects, for instance the suitcase, or the actors holding the rings, from the characters' PoV.

You'll notice that the 'opening' scene of Nathan's entry into the house and him seeing the packed bag in the hallway are shot after the scene in the kitchen: the actor playing Nathan has to do the scene with Julia before he makes his entrance into the house. This just underlines the importance of preparation. In some films you might do the beginning of a scene on one day and the end of it weeks later. I once shot the exterior of a scene in one part of London, then weeks later the interior of the same scene in Spain.

There may be all kinds of reasons for doing the kitchen scene before the hallway – the daylight, sound problems in the hall and so on. Just remember that films are shot according to the needs of the camera, lighting and production. Keeping the emotional truth alive and consistent is the actor's job: you must never complain that going out of sequence is upsetting the flow of your performance, but focus on making the moment truthful and real, every time the slate is shot.

This is how the finished scene would be edited together.

You can see that the above sequence, that will last less than two minutes in the film, would take at least four hours to shoot. That is because each set-up (slate) has to be relit and, although this might be quite a subtle change, even the simplest movement or change of lens on the camera takes time.

Exercise: Watching the Slates

I want you to watch one of your favourite films or television programmes. Choose three consecutive scenes and make a note of each time you see the slate change – not only when the editor cuts from one shot to another but when one slate returns to itself. For example, the scene might open on a wide shot of the detectives driving up to the house, then cut to a medium shot as they walk towards the house, and then return to the wide shot as they enter the house. In that case they would have gone from slate one to slate two, and back to slate one.

You'll be surprised how quickly you can begin to deconstruct scenes into the slates the director has chosen. It's also interesting to see which slates are favoured in the final edit. You'll begin to notice that certain takes are favoured. The more you do this, the clearer will be your understanding of the way film and television is shot.

Film is a series of moments. Think of them as a mosaic; each slate a tile that will make up the whole picture.

Summary

- The actor will work with the director on the blocking of the scene, then the director will shoot in the order that is most efficient for the lighting of the scene.

- You might do the beginning and end of the scene without doing the middle.

- Each slate places the camera in a new position or moves it in another way. Each is another opportunity to reveal your thoughts to camera.

Continuity

There are two types of continuity in film and television.

One is continuity of performance; sustaining your imagination so that you can keep repeating the scene truthfully. The other type is practical. On which line of dialogue did I pick my glass up? When did I drink? Which hand did I pick my napkin up with?

Having a grip on both is essential because the director has two stages in which to make every scene work. The first is in the heat and pressure of the shoot, the second in the calm and concentrated atmosphere of the editing suite. On the floor of the shoot, the director is always pushing for the next shot, the next set-up, because they know they have to get one useable take from each slate. At the same time, they are besieged by a hundred different demands, and it's not until the calm of the edit that the director really sees the bigger picture. During the shoot their concentration is on the principal action and actors, but in the edit they see everything, and the one thing that they become acutely aware of is the actors' continuity. As a director you are always grateful to the actor with good continuity. Cutting their scenes is easy, but those of an actor with poor continuity can be a nightmare. You are constantly looking for shots that match, but their head is at a different angle in different slates or they move at different speeds in different takes. They pick up a glass in their right hand in one take and in their left in the next... But get it right and in the edit the director really notices.

We will concentrate first on continuity of performance, although if you get that right the other, more practical, continuity will follow naturally.

Actors have to sustain their performances throughout the shooting process. Slate after slate, doing the same thing each time but still keeping it fresh and real. They also have to repeat the same physical actions, remembering their own continuity. So if you're playing Nathan in our little scene, and in the first wide shot you scratch your head just after you enter the kitchen, then you are going to have to scratch your head in the medium shot and in the close-up. What seemed natural and easy the first time you did it may subsequently become awkward, clumsy and false with repetition, unless you sustain these physical actions with real thoughts.

So how do you do this? Again we start with your thought process. Say you are the actor playing Nathan. The actress playing Julia turns and makes eye contact with you on the line 'I've decided I'm leaving.'

In that moment, all the pain of her decision to leave her husband is in her eyes. Nathan realises that the thing he has dreaded has now happened. How does he deal with the thought that his wife is really leaving him and all the consequences that flow from that? Perhaps he thinks he can persuade her to stay. Perhaps he thinks that she is a bitch for leaving him. These decisions are yours to make. Perhaps the pain of her leaving is too much. He feels his throat tighten, tears prick his eyes. Instinctively he wants to hide these reactions. If you were to attach a physical movement to this desire for concealment, the almost involuntary act of putting your hand up to shield your mouth would be natural.

Many actors think that the eyes carry the most information and forget that the mouth can convey a good deal of feeling. The eyes carry thought and the mouth carries the emotion.

So the physical movement of shielding an emotional swallow, and the tightening of his lips as he starts to become upset, are part of the character's thought line, and you should be able to sustain that gesture through all the slates.

Already, even before we break the scene down in detail, you are beginning to make choices.

That's why screen acting is an art and not a craft, because the choices you make will be totally different from mine. Continuity in the scene between Julia and Nathan is obviously simple, but if it's not sustained by a thought line you can soon get into trouble. For the actor playing Julia, she might put the wedding ring down as soon as Nathan enters the kitchen, or she might put it down before she gets up to leave. The choice is hers, but if she keeps changing her thought line she might put the ring down in different places in the various shots, and that will restrict what the director and editor can do in the edit. Similarly, if you get up from the chair in the close-up more quickly or slowly than you did in the tracking shot, it will be impossible to cut between the two. Many a good acting moment is lost because of the actor's failure to keep their own continuity.

Mind map of moments

One of the most common questions I am asked is how to sustain continuity in a dynamic emotional scene, one that demands passion and complex emotional shifts. Remember that the scene itself will be broken into different slates and you'll have to do it many times. The actors arrive on set having done all their extensive preparation on the script. They know their thought lines, objectives, and actions, but all of that is prep. Once you arrive at the location or the set, your job is to bring all that work to life. But of course you won't have seen the location before, or worked with the other actors. That speech you have at the beginning of the scene, you might be asked to do while clearing the table of dirty dishes. So be alert.

I ask the actors to run the scene with me directing them, giving them moves and things to do as well as motivating the performances. The scene is suddenly electric. The actors find new thoughts; emotions are surging through their performances because they are now working with other actors.

Then everything stops while the DoP lights the scene. When we return to shoot the scene an hour later, what seemed natural and instinctive in the run-through suddenly becomes stilted. Natural movements, like slapping a hand against a door, can seem suddenly 'theatrical'. That witty speech you give at the end of the dinner party can get very tired and flat by the end of a twelve-hour shooting day.

So how do you sustain the truth and emotional spontaneity of the scene?

By using a 'mind map of moments'. After running the scene with the director, with the blocking complete and the director happy with what you are doing, there is always a period when the DoP relights.

Use this time well. Some actors just drift around the set gossiping, or sit in their trailer texting or chatting with friends. This will only dissipate your energy.

Stay focused.

Find a quiet space and concentrate on what you just did in the run-through. In television you won't have very long to do this, but with practice you will get better at it. While the run-through is still vivid in your mind, make a map of the crucial moments in your memory. Go through the scene in your mind. Now you know exactly where you'll be standing and when and what the other actors will be doing to your character. Place the key moments in a logical line. The moment when another actor startled you with something they did. The moment you went to fill the kettle. Why do you fill the kettle at that point? Even if it's just a move to help give the scene shape, you have to place it in your thought/action line. The moment that you became upset because you didn't know how to deal with the pain the other character made you feel. Position it all in your thought line. Soon you will have a simple list of moments, some driven by your thoughts and others created by your reactions to the other characters. Focus on this narrative of thoughts and moments, running it through your mind many times so that when you return to the set you know where every moment is and how you will sustain them imaginatively.

Directors want to get the best from their actors, but financial and practical constraints often mean that in the end they are reliant on the actors' skills.

Life on Screen

I once made a film about a man called Terry being given a new identity on leaving prison after having committed a horrendous crime as a child. The new identity was supposed to prevent vigilantes discovering where he lived and killing him.

In one scene Terry calls his social worker to ask him if he can tell his new girlfriend his true identity. The social worker is amazed and shocked but believes he can convince Terry of the stupidity of what he is doing.

The scene was set in the early morning, so I had the social worker talking on his mobile, getting dressed as he moved down the stairs so as to keep the conversation private from his wife and family. Their conversation lasted all the way to the bottom of the stairs. It was then that Terry, unconvinced by the social worker's various tactics to persuade him, says that he is definitely telling his new girlfriend about the crime he committed as a child.

In the run-through of the scene, the actor playing the social worker became enraged with Terry, slamming his fist hard against the wall in frustration. It worked well so we kept it in. The conversation with Terry on the stairs was to be shot in one moving shot with a Steadicam, and the angry outburst on another slate in the hallway at the bottom of the stairs. However, the

Steadicam equipment for the long tracking shot on the stairwell had yet to arrive on set, and logistical factors meant we had to shoot the end of the scene first.

This meant the actor, stepping off the stairs into the hallway, had only one line of dialogue on the phone before he became suddenly enraged and hit the wall. He didn't have the emotional advantage of having done the bulk of the scene during which he slowly loses patience with Terry. At the start of this slate he had to be seen to be at the very edge of his character's tipping point, so that his sudden rage felt real and the hitting of the wall not just a theatrical gesture but a real action generated by real frustration. He also had to step into the hallway at the right speed, and at the right stage of dressing, to match the shots that he had yet to do.

The actor was very experienced and had the moments mapped. On 'action' he took the last few steps into the hallway at just the right speed, annoyed at his client but prepared to deal patiently with him. He cleverly matched his dressing to the emotional subtext: as the conversation with Terry became ever more irritating, so the social worker became more irritated with his shirt buttons. Stepping into the hallway from the stairs, he made that the moment in which he started to knot his tie. On the first twist of the tie he heard the news and, bang – his patience snapped. He lost patience with dressing and with Terry at the same time. Wanting to swear, yell that Terry was being a fool, he exploded and hit the wall in anger.

The other slate of the social worker's scene also presented a challenge. The actor had to dress as he descended the stairs, talking discreetly on his mobile whilst buttoning up his shirt, and all this with a film crew in front of him. Although it wasn't bursting with big emotional moments, the scene demanded that he reveal some very complex emotions whilst remembering to do the shirt buttoning and tie knotting exactly the same way on each take.

The actor had done all his preparation on the part but had no idea how or where I would set the scene. The script just said that he was at home when Terry called him. I chose the location because I wanted to add some movement and interest to a very 'talkie' scene. The actor didn't know, either, that I was going to add the dressing routine.

With that sort of complex action, the only way to guarantee continuity is to practise. Find a quiet spot and practise putting the shirt on, and then the tie. Do this with whatever costume or prop you have to deal with in the scene, even if it's as simple as putting on a wristwatch. In the pressured environment of a film set, a strange watch can turn into a snake in a nervous hand.

Practise, but always remember to ask permission. Ask the standby props person if you can borrow the props or, if it's a costume, ask the wardrobe department. If you were doing the social-worker scene, they probably wouldn't want you working with the real shirt because it would have to look clean and pressed for the take, but they would always give you another to work with.

Many a film star has rearranged the furniture in their hotel suite so that they can rehearse the intricate movements of an eating scene.

But getting to be at ease with the physical actions or business of the scene is useless to you unless you can join it to your thought/action line. You have to combine the thought line of the character with the physical actions, using both to reveal the scene's subtextual moments.

Continuity when crying

Another question frequently posed about emotional continuity involves crying on camera. When should you release your tears?

There's little point in bursting into tears when the camera is on the other actor and all that is being recorded of your performance is your shoulder.

But that doesn't mean that when the camera is on the other actor you can just walk through the scene; far from it, it just means you save your true intensity for when the camera is on you. The other actor is dependent on your truthful reaction so they can move on to their next moment. Remember that, in the edit, the director and editor will have to match your performance from the front, where we see your face, to the one where we only see your shoulder. So many times the actor gives a stunning performance to camera, only to let themselves down in the reverse. As they leaned forward and cried in their close-up, their shoulders shook. They wiped the tears from their face and shuddered as they took in deep gulps of air. On the reverse, when only their shoulder is in shot, none of the above happens with the same intensity. Consequently, it's difficult to find a good place to cut to the other person's reaction to your crying. And remember, the reaction to your tears is as important as your crying.

If it doesn't match, the editor will have to search through the rushes – the raw footage from a day's shooting – to find a moment where your crying is not so emotional, so that they can cut away to the reaction shot. In effect, the editor and director are no longer picking the best parts of your performance but the bits that they can cut to. Lack of continuity, therefore, means that your best acting may not make the final edit.

The only way to guarantee that you remember these things is with your 'mind map of moments'. Each major moment of the scene as you have just played it is placed and fixed in your memory so that, even if you only have to run a fragment of the scene again, you know how you played it and where the moments are in relation to each other. If you attach physical movements to moments and thoughts, you are less likely to forget them.

An actor is primarily someone who remembers things. On the most basic level, you remember lines and moves. On a higher level you remember the subtext of a situation; you understand how the undercurrents in life can affect a person. You remember emotional states and how, as an actor, you can adapt and use these insights for your characters. So, remember the construction of a scene, remember how it fits within the overall thrust of the story. Remember what the other actors did in the run-through. Remember what you did and when you did it. Remember why it felt so good. Remember why a certain moment was so poignant; which moment was a bit flat and needed more life. Acting is memory in action.

Going wrong

What do you do if your continuity is perfect but another actor gets it wrong? A bar scene, for instance, where the beer bottle is handed to you two lines early, or your glass is filled a couple of lines later than before?

Just keep going. Whatever you do, don't stop. As with everything else in film and television, you have to adapt to survive. Just concentrate on your own continuity, and try to make it work.

I've seen any number of actors' performances suffer because they don't remember their own continuity. They do the scene; they are doing well; I walk onto the set, give them a note, return to my monitor. Then I see the continuity person giving the actor a list of corrections. And the next take is useless. All I see is an actor worrying about when to pick up the knife, when to hand over the plate. If you want to be good on camera, make it your business to remember your continuity.

Tips for Continuity

- After you have run the scene with the other actors, put together a 'mind map of moments'. Attach these moments to your thought line.

- Practise bits of business with props and costume off the set, but ask permission first. Mime it if necessary. Never play with props on set. Don't touch them until you are actually shooting, or you've been given permission to rehearse with them.

- Do not play with your costume, jewellery or your make-up between takes.

- If you are in doubt about something you did in a take, ask the continuity supervisor.

- If you changed a line or did something differently, tell the 1st AD or continuity. Sometimes it won't matter, but at other times it might.

- Before each slate, remind yourself what happened just before the moment you are about to shoot.

- Remind yourself of what your character wants at this particular moment in the scene.

Eyelines

When you set up for a shot the director will ask you to take your eyelines for the scene. This means the eyelines that your character uses most frequently during the scene. For example, in the previous scene, the actor playing Julia would look down at her ring and then over her shoulder at Nathan. The actor playing Nathan would look at Julia's head, then up to the ceiling, down at the floor, then into the hallway. You are being asked this so that the DoP can check that the light is reflecting in your eyes. After you've been asked to take your eyelines there might be a short pause as the DoP refocuses the lights.

You also have acting eyelines, when you'll be looking outward from the set. Let's say you're shooting in a bar. You are deep in conversation with another character. You stare into the middle distance as your character remembers something sparked off by what they are being told. As you do this, off-set you see a make-up girl chatting with a runner or, worse, a spark flicking through a newspaper. In these circumstances you are within your rights to ask the 1st AD to clear your acting eyelines. Do not feel that you might be seen as a prima donna or particularly demanding. Your job is tough and needs your total concentration. You are a professional. If something in the background distracts you, it might hinder your performance. Just as the DoP wouldn't shoot a scene through a dirty lens, you should not have your concentration broken by unnecessary people in your eyeline.

But please be discreet. Don't make a scene, but tell the 1st AD quietly after the take.

Remember too, sometimes people might have to be in your eyeline. Maybe they're holding equipment essential for the shot or they are needed on standby nearby. They should still respect your need for concentration, but in this case you have to exercise a bit of tolerance.

Eye contact

Inexperienced screen actors will generally hold too much eye contact with the other actors in a scene. This is because the bulk of their experience is in stage acting, where actors fix their eyes on each other and feed each other emotionally throughout a scene.

In film and television, where you are not engaging with the audience's imagination as you would in theatre, your eye contact with the other characters should be as exactly as it is in real life. Here we rarely hold prolonged eye contact, except for the big emotional moments of our lives – 'I love you' or 'I hate you!' – where we need to know what impact this is having on the other person. The better you know someone, the more unlikely it is that you will stare deeply into their eyes. The great British screen actor/director Charles Laughton made it a rule that the actors look at each other as little as possible.

That doesn't mean that you don't make eye contact in a scene but, just as with your 'mind map of moments', you select where and what you look at in the scene, including the other actors. It's best to bounce your eyes off the other character's eyes just as we do in real life, where we quickly scan people's faces to get an idea of their thinking. What you look at, and how, is one of the most revealing things you can do on screen. Here's an example:

We are in a crowded restaurant. The pretty waitress shows the husband and wife to an empty table. As the wife sits, the husband throws a quick glance at the waitress. Their eyes meet, and then the moment is broken as the waitress hands the wife a menu.

Without going into any detail, we understand immediately that something is going on between the waitress and the husband. The wife knows they are having an affair but doesn't want anyone else to know. So, in this tiny scene, where, when and at what these three characters look has to reveal a lot of subtext.

If the actress playing the wife arrives at the restaurant table and just sits down and studies the menu, little will be revealed. But if she catches the discreet look between the husband and the waitress and buries her hurt, she has revealed something that moves the story on. Likewise, if, after exchanging looks with the waitress, the husband sits down and then glances at his wife to see if she has noticed anything, something more is revealed.

The writers have created this scenario for you to bring it to life, and you understand that, without a word being said. What you do with your eyes is very important.

This complex yet subtle ballet of eye movements is very revealing of both story and character. So, as with the previous section, once you have run the scene with the director and taken on board their observations, you must add eyelines to your 'mind map of moments', joining together your inner thought line with the physical actions, including where and what you look at.

Now we know that where and when you look can reveal a lot about the story, the characters' actions and what they want. But what about your character's internal dialogue, their inner thinking?

Eye movements

Extensive research has been done by scientists and psychologists about eye movements and what they reveal about human behaviour. Perhaps we should take a moment to examine it and see how it might help you.

If a person's eyes move up and to the left, they are *remembering* something.

If a person's eyes move up and to the right, they are *imagining* something, creating an image.

If a person's eyes move down and to the left, they are thinking about *themselves* in an objective and sometimes abstract manner. They might be talking about themselves.

If a person's eyes move down and to the right they are thinking about their *feelings*, their emotional state.

If a person's eyes move across to the right with no upward or downward motion they are trying to *reconstruct* a sound.

If a person's eyes move across to the left, they are trying to *remember* a sound.

All these insights can help you develop your character, especially when you have a speech to prepare. Eyeline is clearly very revealing.

The same is true with looking and not looking. Say a character is about to tell their partner they are leaving them.

Their choice of when to have eye contact with the other person is vitally important.

These choices of when and where you look are entirely yours.

I'll use a perennial television and film cliché scene to illustrate the point. In any scene, when the moment comes for the murderer to be revealed, make sure that your character is looking somewhere other than at the murderer. Look at anything or anyone else. This means you can react to the name, then turn your head and look at the murderer when the name is revealed. Now we have both your reaction to the murderer being revealed, and then the glance that shows what your character thinks of the murderer. Actors who think they can just react instinctively and capture the dramatic moments without planning their eyelines are fooling themselves.

Never look down so far that the camera can't see your eyes. If you have to read a newspaper in a scene, for instance, try to read the top of the page, not the bottom.

That way you can reveal what your character is thinking. If your eyes are hidden, there is little you can reveal. Likewise, if you are reading legal documents or a letter, make sure you angle them so that the camera can see your eyes and your reaction to what you are reading.

Getting direction

Sometimes, when you have first run your scene, the direc
tor might ask you to look at a certain character at a precise
moment (or at an object or, indeed, into a particular place
in thin air). Make sure that you have a clear idea of what the
director is after: don't be afraid to ask why and what you are
looking at.

For example, I was recently directing an actress playing a
prisoner talking to her lawyer. I asked her to look away from
the lawyer in the middle of his big speech because in the edit
I intended to insert a flashback to the night of the crime. Just
reading the text, however, the actress would never have
known that I was doing that.

Similarly, when you are doing blue- or green-screen work,
where characters and backgrounds are added digitally after
shooting, you will be asked to take a variety of eyelines. Sometimes you might have to imagine that the tennis ball on a stick
that you're looking at is an alien monster, and the tiny red spot
of light on the backdrop is an incoming spaceship. Make sure
you ask where each eyeline is directed and calibrate your performance accordingly. Many actors overstate the difficulty of
working with green-screen, but for me it's just a matter of
applying your imagination. Any actor worthy of the name
should be able to imagine an off-screen monster!

Any eyeline that the director gives you, you must follow. But
don't let that stop you also deciding for yourself what to look
at and when to look at it.

At the end of a take, very often an excellent one, the director
will start directing you from the monitor. That is, they will
give you verbal commands such as 'Look up'... 'Look at the
light'... 'Stare into the empty cup'... 'Look back at the door.'

Do not be disturbed by this. They are just covering themselves by recording different eyelines to use in the edit. They
will do this particularly after a good take because the actor

is completely 'in the zone' – mentally focused. Or it might be that they intend to move on so are getting as many options for the edit that they can. When you do these eye-lines, back them up with thoughts. For instance, the director asks you to look back at the door: this is the door that your husband, the husband you are about to leave, is coming through. Perhaps you had never looked at the door during the take and the director wants a shot to use when you hear your husband entering the hallway. The more you give the director, the greater range of options you offer in the edit, and the more screen time you, the actor, will get overall.

Blinking

Everyone has a different blink rate, depending on what they are doing and what they are feeling. The more agitated and nervous we feel, the greater the blink rate. Calm and alone, we barely blink.

For an actor on set, blinking can reveal nerves. A high blink rate during a scene can alert the director and the other actors to the fact that that actor is not assured or comfortable. It can also make for difficulty in the edit: an old editing adage says you never cut on a blink.

On the other hand, an unblinking stare can be deeply unnerving, as there is something inhuman about it. As Hannibal 'The Cannibal' Lecter in *The Silence of the Lambs*, Anthony Hopkins famously never blinks. Conversely, Jodie Foster, playing Agent Starling, blinks very effectively. Despite her putting on a brave face, Lecter's laser-like analysis is making her deeply nervous, and as much as she tries not reveal her fear by blinking, she cannot help herself and consequently blinks harder than ever. Robert Powell, as Jesus in *Jesus of Nazareth*, also chose not to blink so as to differentiate the character from those around him. Those are the two extremes, blinking too much and not blinking at all.

I always tell actors that if they have confidence in what they are doing, do their prep and enter the moment completely, blinking will become entirely natural to the character. However, there are ways a blink can enhance certain character and situations.

The 'slow cut-out blink' means that a person keeps their eyelids closed for longer than normal. This is useful for revealing that a character is of high status, or at least thinks they are and should be respected. By cutting out what they see, they appear indifferent to what people think of them.

Likewise the cut-out blink is highly effective when your character has just received news that they don't want to accept. The death of a loved one, perhaps, or the length of their prison sentence.

The sudden glazed stare can indicate that a person has disappeared into their own world and is ignoring what the other characters are saying. This suggests that what has just happened or been said has had a deep impact or them.

A quick glance is always handy for use in the edit. An editor always needs something to cut to as a character says a line. If your character throws a quick glance at the person speaking, or the person being spoken to, you will gain more screen time. George Clooney does this very effectively, always moving his head and eyelines, giving the editor and director something to work with.

Tips for Eyelines

- Pick your eyelines for dramatic effect, for example when the murderer is about to be revealed.

- Your eyelines need not always be on another character. Often we stare into the middle distance when lost in thought.

- Beware of looking down too much.
- Do not hold the eyeline of other characters unless absolutely necessary. A fixed eyeline is one-dimensional, unless that is what the scene calls for.
- Keep it simple. If you have hundreds of different eyelines in the scene it will be impossible to cut.
- Eyelines are important as moves. Remember them.

Frame Sizes

There are four major frame sizes that the screen actor has to be aware of. To make them clear, I'll show you a little scene with all four lens sizes.

Wide, master or establishing shots

This covers your entire body from the top of your head to your toes.

Obviously, in the wide you have to be as natural as you are in the other shots but the energy you use can be greater That energy passes into your body and consequently into your gestures. The wide is very often a guide track for the editor.

Mid-shots

A mid-shot is from your waist up to the top of your head, and is the most common shot in television drama.

This is because you can place two or three characters within the frame and record all the dialogue and action. You then have the scene covered in terms of storytelling. Any extra close-ups or cut-aways are saved for the most important moments. Until quite recently, television was driven by dialogue – 'radio with pictures' is how one producer described it. But with bigger budgets, especially from companies like Netflix, HBO and Sky, television is now very often shot more adventurously than many films.

Close-ups (CU)

Shot from the shoulder line up to the top of the head, this frame is used a lot in film because it's the one in which the character can most reveal their thinking to camera.

Within a close-up, the actor's eyes should be about three-quarters of the way up the frame. Star actor Paul Newman once described the close-up as 'one of the most important inventions of the twentieth century'. In a way I think he's right. For the first time an actor could reveal in detail what he or she was thinking without resorting to dialogue. Steve McQueen would famously go through scripts cutting out huge swathes of dialogue, saying simply that he could do it better with a look in close-up. It was no accident that he became such a huge film star.

Knowing the frame size is important because it calibrates the degree of energy and intensity you need for the shot.

In short: the wide shot gives context to the scene; the mid-shot carries information about what is happening; and the close-up reveals the character's thoughts. The wide shot shows your whole body, so you should focus most of your energy here. Close-up is where you can reveal your character's private thoughts to camera; the equivalent of a soliloquy in the theatre.

Here's an example from a short film that I shot called *UXB*. Set during the Second World War, it's about a bomb-disposal officer having an affair with the landlady of his digs. This scene is from the beginning of the film, when the audience don't yet know what our leading man does for a living.

In the wide, we see the bomb-disposal officer arriving at the scene of an unexploded bomb. We see the warning signs and the other two soldiers who have prepared the site for the officer. We see that he has higher rank and high status.

In the mid-shot we see him looking down a stairwell at something.

In the next mid-shot we see the other soldiers ducking down behind a wall of sandbags, preparing the radio with which they will communicate with the officer.

In the next shot we see the officer bending down to examine the unexploded bomb.

Then the close-up as he prepares to defuse it.

Each shot demands a subtly different kind of energy from the actor.

The frame size decides the amount of energy you need to put into your body. As the frame gets tighter, you should intensify your thoughts and reactions while restricting large arm and body movements.

Filming the above scene would involve every frame size. The actor has to do the same thing in each frame size or it won't match in the edit. So what do they do differently?

In the wide they should behave just as they would in real life, just with a little more energy. In real life, most people's body movements are quite muted, but in film and television, where you are telling a story, you need some movement and action in the wide to hold the audience's attention.

In the mid-shot, the officer looking down the stairwell should concentrate on being completely natural. In the close-up of his face he should intensify his thinking, revealing his inner monologue, his anxiety. It would be crass to reveal this by drumming his fingers, but he could perhaps bite his lip.

Extreme close-ups

An extreme close-up takes in your face from your mouth to just above your eyebrows.

In extreme CU, every detail of your face, from the expression in your eyes to the way you hold your mouth, shows your inner mental and emotional state. In this scenario, it would indicate the extreme stress of pulling out the fuse, perhaps just with a twitch of the officer's eyelid. You can also have an over-shoulder CU, which is where the back of the other character's head and shoulder are on the edge of the frame.

So how do you, as the actor, know the size of the frame?

The best way is watch the boom operator. They dip their boom mic into the shot to find 'edge of frame'. If you watch this you will see exactly the shape of the frame and you'll be able to judge the energy of your performance accordingly.

Don't be deceived into thinking that the closer the camera is, the closer the shot. Sometimes a director will use an 85mm lens and have the camera ten metres away from you, and you will be in a big close-up. Or if the director uses a 25mm lens and the camera is ten metres away from you, you will be in a wide shot.

If in doubt, ask – generally, miming a frame size to the DoP or the camera operator will elicit an answer. After all, the DoP doesn't want his shot messed up by you making gestures which turn out to be outside the frame, just because you didn't know the size.

Always remember that as an actor on a shoot you are a member of a big team, and everyone there wants you to do your best.

The line (or the 180-degree rule)

You will hear a lot about this on film and television sets. The 'line' is simply which side of the actor the director is deciding to shoot from.

In a two-shot, when two characters are talking in a static scene, this is relatively simple. You put the camera over actor A's right shoulder to shoot actor B. Then over actor B's left shoulder when the reverse is shot.

This is so that the eyelines will match on screen and it will appear that actor A is looking into actor B's eyes. If we shot the same scene but did the reverse over actor A's right shoulder, it would appear on screen as if the actors were looking away from each other, as in the two photos below:

Or if the director crosses the line, the eyelines look wrong, as below:

I believe that on the whole, actors should concentrate on their job of making the character work in the scene, and not concern themselves with the technical aspects of the line. In a large scene with many characters this can be very complex, especially when you add movement and the director might have a portion of the scene shot one side of the line and another part shot on the other side.

Actors new to film and television often like to hide their inexperience by talking about 'the line' when you are setting up the shot and blocking the scene. Let me tell you, this is both time-consuming and annoying, so my advice is, concentrate on what you are doing – being the character in the situation.

Dirty or clean frames

'Do you want the frame dirty or clean?' is a question from the DoP to the director, and just means, when shooting over an actor's shoulder, 'Do you want a bit of the actor in the frame ("dirty") or not ("clean")?'

Depending on the director's answer, the DoP or the 1st AD will ask you to put your weight either on your left or your right. This simply means leaning slightly to that side in order to get yourself in or out of the frame. Remember, everything is being done so that the scene looks good on screen. So even if you are leaning over to the left and straining to make eye contact with the other actor, you have to find a way to make it work.

Dialogue

Not overlapping dialogue

In everyday speech, dialogue naturally overlaps: rarely do we wait for the other person to stop talking before we reply. In film and television, however, it has generally been considered advisable not to do it, although this has changed a bit in the last few years and many young directors do not seem to mind actors overlapping. Either way, you should prepare yourself not to overlap your dialogue.

When you run dialogue with a friend, especially if it is a fast-talking scene or, most commonly, an argument, leave a tiny pause before saying your line. Keep the thought and impulse clear in your mind but practise leaving that tiny pause before you speak.

This will feel odd when you first start doing it but the director will thank you when it comes to the edit.

Not overlapping helps the editor when they are putting the scene together. If your dialogue is always overlapping the other character's, it makes it very difficult to cut to alternate takes. In much more radical edits, where a whole chunk of the scene is cut away to make the story clearer or to make the film shorter, overlapping presents big difficulties.

Practise by learning an argument from a film or television drama. Get a friend to read in the other lines, then run the scene at speed with no overlapping. Just leave a tiny gap – if it's too long it will make the scene feel false and throw the other actors.

Pick-ups

This happens when an actor has dried, or something has gone wrong in a take. The 1st AD will say 'Let's pick the scene up from...' and quote the line of dialogue from which you'll be starting again. The shooting process will be called: 'Turn over, speed, rolling, mark it!' The clapper will then be marked with PU1 and on 'action' you'll start again from the pick-up line and go through to the end.

While the shot is being reset, it's important that you remain clear about where the scene is going from the pick-up point. If you were in the middle of an emotional crescendo, you have to be able to recreate that emotional state. Remind yourself, too, where you were looking at the pick-up point. If you are unsure about continuity, just ask.

These days television is shot so quickly that one or two takes is the most an actor can expect, so you'll almost certainly be doing lots of pick-ups as things go wrong.

Drying

It happens. Despite all the prep, something just throws you and you lose the line. Or perhaps the director asks you to say a familiar line in a completely different way. And you dry. What should you do?

Just take a moment and think. Can you remember the line? If you can, carry on. Actors dry all the time, so don't get yourself into a terrible state thinking that you'll never work again.

If you can't remember the line, apologise and ask to be reminded. Either the continuity person will give you the line or the director will call cut so that you can have a look at the script to remind yourself.

It is my belief that if you have done all your prep it is nearly impossible for you to dry or drop a line. Where it can happen to you is on a long-running series, where after a few months of diligent work you fall into bad habits and just skim the lines without doing the necessary amount of prep. Once you've been on a series for a couple of episodes you probably don't have to do the same level of prep you'd do on a one-off drama, but you should still be doing it.

If you start drying on set, it's a sign that you are not doing enough work on the script.

Hitting Marks

In film and television, your movements must be slowed so that the camera can follow the action. Even if you have to leap up from a chair, you do it ten per cent more slowly, because the camera has to be able to follow you. And despite what people say, the camera lies. One of the things it does is speed up action. Let's say you're walking down a corridor talking to a doctor. You have to talk fast but move slowly, partly because you have an entire film crew in front of you but also because of the way the lens distorts the action.

'Hitting your mark' is the technical term for when you have to find the same spot in the scene. The place will usually be marked on the floor with a piece of tape, but you'll some-times encounter a sausage-shaped doorstop filled with sand that helps you find your mark by touching it with your foot. Sometimes you will be given several marks in one scene.

It's crucial that you hit your mark precisely, because if you don't you will be out of focus and the shot will be unusable. You must also hit your marks without looking as if you stopped because you had to, and you can't look down to see if you've hit it. You must do it naturally within the rhythm of the scene, making the way you stop real for your charac-ter. If you stop bang on your mark but look as if you stopped for no logical reason, it will look false and the audience will not be convinced.

So how do you do it?

Never stop mid-thought. Find a logical reason for your character to stop moving. In the scene from *Somebody's Father*, why does Nathan stop where he does at the back of the kitchen? After all, his marriage is in trouble, his whole family is falling apart. He might want to confront his wife, in which case he would go and sit opposite her and say, 'Why have you packed? Are you leaving me?' But in this case, the director has asked you to stop at the back of the kitchen – because it makes a better picture.

It tells the story the director wants to tell, and it's what the director wants you to do. So you have to be able to take the preparation you have done and adapt it to the blocking that you have been given.

So, you've done your prep for the scene and you enter the kitchen wanting to say, 'Why have you packed your bags?' After all, it would make perfect sense. But your mark is at the back of the kitchen, and from there you can't see the face of the actress playing Julia. What you do, then, is give yourself a good reason why Nathan doesn't say it. When you enter you see her sitting with her back to you. She doesn't turn and say anything. Nathan might think, 'I've seen her bag in the hall… She's going to leave me! If I confront her she might use my aggression to get angry and then she will definitely leave me. How can I talk her out of leaving me? Because if she does leave me now… I fear I will completely break down.'

So at what point in that inner stream of thought would Nathan stop moving?

When she doesn't turn round as he enters the kitchen.

Why then?

Because the fact that she doesn't turn or speak as he enters the kitchen sends a big signal in terms of body language.

Remember that we are visual animals: body language accounts for a good deal of the way we communicate with each other. In 1971, Professor Albert Mehrabian of the University of Los Angeles did a comprehensive study of the way people communicate with each other. The professor's tests revealed the following formula, which has been proven again and again since the seventies.

Of the three major groups that we use to communicate with each other – words, voice and body language – body language accounted for by far the largest part, at a huge 55%. Vocal tone, pitch and word pace accounted for 38% of the information we get from each other. And finally, the words themselves made up a tiny 7%.

When I heard Professor Mehrabian being interviewed, he expressed his annoyance at the many authors of 'body language' books who have misused the above statistic. What those figures relate to is 'emotional' communication. If you want your blue socks from the bottom drawer of the chest of drawers that are in the third bedroom on the right, you need spoken language to communicate that information.

So the above statistic does work for the screen actor, where very often what you are saying has little or nothing to do with what your character really feels.

How do you naturalise finding your mark? Well, you can find your own position in relationship to the furniture. For instance, the actor playing Nathan might find his mark by stopping just as he passes the second cabinet door. Or there might be a prop on the kitchen worktop by which to judge your position. You then time your thinking to that mark. So your stopping when Julia does not turn when you enter the kitchen is both real and in the moment, each time that you do it.

Stepping onto a mark

This is where you will be asked just to take a step onto your mark.

The actor playing Julia will have to step onto her mark when she stops in the doorway as she is leaving. This type of mark is used for close-up shots. The best way to hit this is to stand on the mark and take one step backwards. Then, on 'action', one step forward – and you cannot miss the mark. If the distance to hit your mark is further, just adjust the number of steps back and forwards.

This is a technical solution, but it will not work unless the stopping point is supported by a thought. For Julia in the doorway, the thought could be:

'Am I doing the right thing? Perhaps I should stay and see him through the next few days… I can't. I simply cannot stay with Nathan while he continues to stand by his father…'

She would then move off and wipe frame.

Swaying into shot

This is where you stand on your mark and are asked to sway or shuffle slightly into shot. What the director wants is a bit of movement so that if they want to cut to this shot in the edit, they don't go from a movement shot to a stationary actor. Because focus is critical, however, they will not ask the actor to actually step into the shot. What you should do here is just adjust your weight from one foot to the other, letting the movement go through your body.

Again, keep focusing on your character's thought process. When you're being asked to do these very technical things, it's easy to forget about this – but remember, without thought the shot might be beautifully focused but it will lack reality.

Turning into shot

This is exactly what it says it is. You turn into the shot. The critical thing is remembering which way you turned when you shot the wide – and remember, there might be hours between the wide and the close-up. The director will assume that you remember and, should you get it wrong, continuity will prompt you, but it's still embarrassing and shows a lack of professionalism.

Sitting into frame

You are asked to sit into the shot. So you start the slate from a standing position, ready to sit down after 'action' has been called. It's as well to check with continuity what you were saying as you sat down in the wide. You might have been halfway through a line when you sat or just after it, or you might have sat during someone else's lines. The director will already have chosen their wide take, so will want to match the close-up to that.

Standing up into shot

Same thing and, again, a quick check with continuity will help. Remember your thought process; that's what generates your moves.

> *Tips for Hitting Marks*
> - Make sure you find a reason driven by thought to stop you on your mark.
> - Try to learn the geography of the scene from the set, and your physical relationship to the other characters. These are constantly being adjusted, so stay alert.
> - Remember the speed at which you do things. If you fall into a chair at speed in the wide, you'll have to replicate this speed in the close-up.
> - Remember your physical movements in the scene, connect them with thought and adjust for frame size.

Teaching screen acting has taught me that just getting someone to hit his or her marks in a technical fashion is almost useless to the modern actor. They learn to do it, but forget everything when faced with a real shoot under the intense pressure of a film set. I have developed the following exercises to stretch you, as much as to teach the nuts and bolts. Again, the more you practise these scenes, the better.

Exercise: Applying Skills

This simple exercise will utilise many of the things you've just read about. You'll need some props for this scene, and you will need to do a lot of preparation on the characters' thinking and motivation before you shoot. The character in the scene can be either male or female, though in the script below has been written as a woman.

Props

- A wine bottle half-full of red fruit juice.
- A mobile phone.
- A simple bunch of flowers.
- An envelope with a card in it. The card has a simple message written in it.

The Situation

You have been invited to your new boyfriend's house for dinner for the first time. You are very much in love. Before you sit down to eat, he has to make a phone call in another room. Then a message comes through on his mobile.

Technical Set-up

The location is a kitchen and I want your camera operator to say one spoken line out of vision and to give you two cues during the scene. These cues should be given, as they would on a real film set, by the director clicking his fingers (they are easily taken out of the soundtrack in post-production). Both the off-screen line and the signals are marked in the script.

The Scene

Alex stands by the table listening as her boyfriend calls from the other room.

                    BOYFRIEND

        Help yourself to wine. I've
        got to make a call from the
        landline.

Alex sits and pours a glass of wine while looking around the kitchen. Alex takes a sip of wine and is impressed by the vintage. The boyfriend's mobile bleeps as a message arrives.

(The camera operator clicks their fingers to indicate the bleep.)

Alex sits looking at the door, listening for her boyfriend, then looks at the phone. Unable to resist, she gets up and looks at the message on the phone.

The message reads 'Thank you for this afternoon. It was great. The card says what I couldn't say!'

The message has been sent from the boyfriend's ex-partner. Unnerved and a little confused by the message, she puts the phone down. She then sees an envelope with a card inside it propped up by the kettle. She wonders if she should look. She listens; in the distance she hears his voice on the phone. Again unable to resist, she goes to the envelope and takes the card out and reads it. The message reads, 'I still love you.' She then hears her boyfriend coming down the hallway.

(*The camera operator clicks their fingers to indicate the boyfriend approaching.*)

Alex replaces the card into its envelope and rushes back to her seat. Once in her seat she calms herself and prepares to greet her boyfriend warmly when she realises that she has left the wine over by the envelope. The boyfriend enters the kitchen and stands by the door. She looks at him, then at the wine that has been left by the envelope.

CUT.

A simple enough scene, but filled with subtext, which you will have to reveal to the camera.

So, having done your preparation on the script, run the scene a few times in your kitchen until you find a physical blocking that is comfortable for you.

Remember, every moment must be motivated by a thought or it will look false. You also have to justify the character's behaviour. Why would you look at a private text message? And then at the message in the card? I know I would never look at someone else's private texts, but this character does. Why? What is it about their life and background that has made them so insecure? Your challenge is to find a motivation that justifies the character's sensibilities.

Once you are comfortable with the blocking of the scene, run through it slowly and have your camera operator mark the four main positions the character takes up. They are:

- The place where you stand at the start of the scene.
- The chair where you sit and pour the wine.
- The place where you read the text message on the phone.
- The place where you read the card.

You mark the chair near the table so that it can be placed back in position at the start of every take. Likewise, the wine bottle and the envelope with the card in it. No matter how many takes you do, you can replace each prop in its exact position.

Now remembering the procedure for shooting:

- 'Standby.'
- 'Turn over.'
- 'Camera speed.'
- 'Sound rolling.'
- 'Mark it.'
- 'Action.'

The Wide Shot (Slate 1)

A wide shot contains the whole actor from the top of their head to their feet. If your kitchen is not big enough to contain this shot, don't worry. Shoot it as a moving mid-shot, one that shows the actor from the waist upwards, leaving a foot or so of space above their head. The camera should follow the action from a fixed point, preferably the kitchen doorway and, if possible, it should be on a tripod.

This is slate 1. Do it at least three times, making sure that you hit your marks and keep your own continuity. Concentrate on those tiny things that in real life we take for granted, such as which way you turn when you hear the boyfriend coming back to the kitchen. Which hand do you pick the wine bottle up in? Which hand do you use to pick up the phone? How do you pick up the envelope? How do you open the card?

Now I want you to shoot three close-ups of specific moments. Remember, in close-up, keep the actor's eyes at the three-quarter point of the frame.

The First Close-up (*Slate 2*)

The first close-up is when your character sits at the table and pours the wine. The phone bleeps as the text arrives. You decide to look at the text, get up and go over to the phone. Make sure your camera operator knows that you are going to wipe frame.

What you must concentrate on here is filling the two key moments while you are sitting. What are you thinking as you pour the expensive wine? Here's your chance to reveal how excited you are by your date – or, for that matter, how anxious you are. How do you feel about your new lover?

Your camera operator will then give you the cue for the text message arriving. The message arrives on the phone. The true reason that you go and look lurks beneath the surface. Perhaps you have fooled yourself into thinking it's just a bit of harmless fun. Whatever your motivation for looking at the text, remember it has to be balanced by your sense that reading it is wrong.

Remember, too, that you sit into this shot. Before 'action', the camera is focused on the position you'll be in once you've sat down. So start out of frame, and on 'action' you enter frame and sit.

If you don't have a chair and table in the kitchen, just find a place where your character would casually lean while waiting for their girlfriend/boyfriend. The important thing is that you start out of the frame and move into it.

The Second Close-up (Slate 3)

This is your character scrambling back into the chair as she hears the boyfriend coming back to the kitchen.

On 'action' you enter frame, sitting quickly and taking on the air of someone who has been waiting patiently. Having done this successfully, you relax. Only then do you realise that you have left your wine glass over by the envelope, thus revealing your guilt.

Obviously, in these exercises we do not shoot the reverses. The reverse would be the boyfriend standing in the doorway smiling, happy to be back and ready to start the evening, only to notice the wine glass by the envelope. He might realise straightaway that you had looked at the card, or he might only realise this later on when he looks at the text. What is unavoidable now, however, is the fact that you have been caught.

It's a great film moment if you can reveal it. It's also a test, because we are filming out of sequence, shooting the end before the middle, just as you would on a real film.

The Third Close-up (Slate 4)

This next close-up is where you read the text on the phone. Again, step into the shot hitting your mark, pick up the phone and read the text. You are disturbed by the tone of it. Then you notice the card by the kettle, wonder if you should read it, decide you are going to. Then you listen to see if your boyfriend is still talking on the phone. Now, followed by the camera, you move to the card and read it. You put the wine glass down near to where the card was. You read the message, realising that your lover has been with his ex. Worse still, his 'ex' still loves him. Then you hear him coming down the hall.

The camera operator gives you another signal. You hastily put the card back into the envelope, put it back on the side and then wipe frame.

'Cut.'

Editing and Evaluating

Should you wish to edit this little scene together, you will need to add three cut-aways to the shooting list: a big close-up of the text message; a close-up on what's written in the card, and a close-up of your character picking the card up and putting it down again. This last cut-away will give you something to cut to after she wipes frame having heard her boyfriend coming back to the kitchen. A close-up of the card with the wine next to it will build the tension in the scene.

As with the other exercises, it would be best if you did this now, before we move on to look at the most common mistakes people make.

The main thrust of the exercise is for you to gain confidence in sitting into shots, hitting your marks and remembering your own continuity. After you've watched the film back, write yourself a list of what you liked about your performance. Give your thoughts a few days to ferment, then do the whole thing again. I think you'll be surprised by your improvement.

Common Pitfalls

The energy of the movement in the wide shot is different from that in the close-up: This is especially true on the second close-up (slate 3), when your character has to rush back to the chair. The actor will dutifully stand beside the chair and, on 'Action', drop into it. In the wide they would have had to run across the room and the energy of their sitting down would have been quite different. The solution is to start further away from the chair. Don't be afraid to ask the director or the 1st AD if you could start from where the card is placed. The same applies to shots in which you have to come through a door, or push away from somebody or something. If you don't feel that the physical energy in the close-up matches that of the wide, ask if there is a way to replicate the wide. Most directors will try to accommodate you, unless there's a very good reason why this isn't possible.

Your continuity is wrong: You pick up the phone with your left hand in the wide, but use your right hand in the close-up. You turn the wrong way when returning to the chair at the end of the scene. The most common fault of all is not coming into the close-up at the right angle. Even experienced actors have been known to sit onto the chair from the wrong side. So if it hasn't gone quite as well as you hoped, just remember you are in good company.

Sometimes you have to get it wrong to get it right.

Voice

Vocal Range

A lot of actors make the mistake of thinking that the voice is less important in screen acting than for the stage, but this couldn't be more wrong.

Voice is central to how you communicate, and for revealing your thoughts and emotion. One crucial mistake that nearly all actors make is that their vocal levels are far too loud. They are still 'projecting' their voices as if they were on stage, whereas in film and television your vocal level should match the size of the frame.

In close-up, you should speak just loudly enough for someone a foot away from your face to hear you. Place your hand a foot from your face and speak to it. You'll be surprised at how little voice you need. In a mid-shot, your voice should be just loud enough to reach someone sitting across from you at the dining table. Imagine someone sitting across the table: behind them, about four feet away, is someone else. I want you to speak so the person opposite hears you, but the person behind them doesn't. In a wide shot, you can speak at your normal level, or as loudly as you think necessary in that particular scene.

A good rule of thumb is to watch where the boom microphone is. If it's a few inches above your head, it must be a close-up. A foot above your head, it must be a mid-shot, and a few feet above your head, it must be a wide. You need never bother anyone by asking the frame size, unless the shot is without sound (MOS).

Radio mics are small microphones attached to your clothing so that they can't be seen on camera. They pick up every
breath you take. Be very careful when you are on radio mics.
The director has wireless earphones and hears everything,
even when the camera is not rolling – I've had many a
chuckle at actors' off-screen conversations. On the other
hand, stories are also legion of directors hearing disparag-
ing remarks about themselves from an unwary actor
(though some may very well deserve it!).

Imagine a scene in which you are talking to a large crowd of
people and it comes to your close-up. What do you do?

Clearly, in the wide shot you would have spoken loudly to
make yourself heard above the noise of the crowd, bearing
in mind that when you are shooting the scene the angry
mob will be completely silent. Their yells, boos and howls
of delight will be added later. When it comes to the mid-
shot, however, you have to reduce the volume and reduce it
even further in the close-up. But lack of volume does not
mean lack of intensity. Quite the reverse. By making it clear
what the character wants, you will not need volume to make
it credible: each line will have its purpose. Some actors use
volume to give reality to their performances, especially during angry rants. But watch Al Pacino in *The Godfather*
series. Watch Russell Crowe in almost anything he does. As
the shot gets closer, they get quieter and more intense.

Too much voice is a common problem on quickly shot television shows. Here the writing can be quite melodramatic,
the situations extreme and the time allotted to shooting far
too short. It's then that the inexperienced actress will
screech, 'Why did you sleep with her? She was my friend!'
Or the inexperienced actor will yell, 'I love her! She makes
me feel like a man!'

Here, volume has replaced the emotional truth that the
characters are feeling. The actors, having had no rehearsal
and now under enormous pressure to get the scene shot,

push themselves into an emotional cauldron. They've run the scene a few times, each time getting louder. The sound man has turned the mic down and within moments the volume spreads among the other cast members, until they're all overemoting vocally. The result is a lot of crude acting. If they had restrained their vocal levels, their energy would have entered into their thinking and created a greater mental matrix of betrayal and confusion that would have shown in their eyes and on their faces. By putting the emotional intensity into their voices, however, performances that seemed good on the floor of the studio are seen to lack credibility when narrowed to the screen.

So, always in film and television – less volume, please.

Sound technicians are always asking actors to 'speak up', which actors, willing to please, interpret as speaking more loudly. In fact, what the sound person really needs is better clarity and focus in the voice. It's impossible to make out what the actor is saying because the dialogue is garbled, or mumbled. But asked to speak up, the actor just starts to project, which makes the sound guy's job easier but the director's much harder. So if the sound technician asks you to speak up, remember: greater clarity and diction come before volume.

Actors in soaps and regular drama series in particular are inclined to sink into a quasi-naturalism. Just like real life but not quite. They try to convince us of this by mumbling and breaking up their lines into what they imagine is a naturalistic way of speaking. The result, however, is a mess. In an effort to appear natural, but not having done enough work on the character and text, they make poor choices about which words to emphasise, break important lines up to pick their teeth, or just look down and mumble and appear natural. Naturalism is a creative cul de sac for the good screen actor.

Life on Screen

I once asked an actor why he was scratching his face during a speech, and he said, 'So it looks believable.'

'But,' I replied, 'You're telling someone about something you saw. Something that could help them.'

'Yeah,' he said, 'But it goes on a bit and I want to make it seem real.'

In his effort to make the speech real, he had made it almost impossible to understand. I'm afraid that television is filled with actors who think they're making a character interesting by covering their mouths when they speak, or looking down all the time.

Naturalism belongs in documentaries and reality television. An actor's job is to turn the character in the script into a real inhabitant of the writer's imaginary world. Make sure that what you are saying in character has clarity. You need it to be heard by the other characters.

'Less voice' does not mean whispering. This is as bad as overprojecting. But using less voice presents a whole set of new problems for actors, because they have been trained to project.

Once you start to use less voice, you risk becoming unfocused and underenergised. Many actors start to struggle once they are asked to bring down their vocal projection, because they are used to energising their performance through their voices. In film and television, the story is carried by your thoughts, and those thoughts are revealed equally through your voice, face and body. Reducing your voice to an ordinary human level almost immediately brings greater reality to your character. Less volume, however, can also lead to less vocal attack if your voice isn't properly warmed up. Inexperienced screen actors often fail to do vocal warm-ups before starting work, but if your voice has not been warmed up properly, you risk losing clarity of diction and, more importantly, flexibility. At the end of this section is a short series of exercises that will help develop your voice, and a series of short vocal warm-ups which you can use before you go on set.

Walking and Talking

Moving and speaking simultaneously is something you have to do all the time in film and television. It's one thing walking along chatting with a friend, quite another walking along playing a complex scene with a film crew moving a few metres in front of you. In these circumstances it's crucial to remember the golden rule of tracking shots:

Walk slow, speak fast.

Wherever in the world you shoot a long 'walkie-talkie' shot, the director will ask you to do the same thing. 'Could you talk a bit faster and walk a little slower?' Should you rush the dialogue? No, absolutely not; just speed it up a bit. I've found that most actors pause too often within their dialogue, taking too long to make the essential psychological gearshifts the scene needs. Once you know that you're going to do a scene on the move, make sure that you always rehearse the dialogue whilst moving. That way the movement of your body and the character's thinking can be knitted together. Pay attention to the speed at which you move. Most of us, and certainly most actors I've worked with, move a little more quickly when anxious. So when you're rehearsing, consciously make yourself move at half-speed but keep the flow of dialogue at normal speed.

When you're actually filming, the camera and grips will start to work more quickly once they are familiar with a shot, so as the takes go on you too can start to pick up speed. The usual rule is to move about ten per cent more slowly than you would in real life.

Tracking shots

There are two ways of doing a long tracking shot. One is by placing the camera on a dolly and pulling the dolly backwards ahead of the actors. If the surface is rough or uneven, they might have to lay a track for the dolly to run on, but this takes time and costs money. It's also awkward for the actors to walk through, because once you start doing a long tracking shot, you have to walk either beside or through the rails. Many a take has been lost to an actor just clipping the edge of the track with their shoe.

The other way of doing a tracking shot is with a Steadicam, and this is beginning to supersede the old system of tracking. Detective series, for example, often open with a scene where the camera seems to float around the characters inspecting a crime scene. That will all have been shot using a Steadicam.

For you, working with either method of tracking is much the same. Rehearse the scene, slowing your movements while keeping your speech at normal pace. Then practise walking the area that you will have to cover in the shot, looking out for obvious hazards. A kerb can suddenly get four inches higher when you've got the crew in front of you.

Character and Accents

The most successful screen actors have centred voices that match their bodies. To find your own voice, you have to speak from your centre, and that really means speaking from your diaphragm. If you speak from your throat, the sound will be strangulated and irritating to listeners. Also, remember that a big television series can be a long shoot and last for six months or more – you'll strain your voice and probably lose it. Lose your voice, mucking up the producer's tight schedule, and they are not going to thank you! Walk and speak from your centre and you can't go wrong.

If you feel your voice rising into your throat, take a moment and recentre yourself.

Vocal levels

Can you shout in a television programme? Whisper on film? Of course you can. You just have to be absolutely sure that that choice is right for your character.

And if you are going to shout, be sure that you do the same thing each time. Once you've rehearsed, the sound engineer will have fixed their various levels for the scene. When you speak quietly, they turn the dials up. When you are loud, they turn them down. So if for some reason you suddenly shout at a point when you were previously quiet, the sound will be lost and you'll have to go again, and no director wants to hear that. In addition, the sound recordist will probably have a raging headache for the rest of the day and blame it on your amateurism.

So keep continuity of your vocal levels.

Finding the character's voice

Most of us have a public voice and a private one. Imagine you are arriving at a dinner party. You are greeted at the door, then taken into a dining room filled with strangers. Even as you walk into the room, you are preparing your voice. You may be shy and find such things a nightmare, in which case your voice will tighten and you probably push the volume too hard. You may be an extravagant character who loves to be the centre of attention, in which case you will be preparing your voice in a different way. But in both cases, a public voice is being prepared.

Now let's analyse the differences between your own public and private voices. Each character you play will have a public and private voice.

Just so that we are clear what a private voice is, it's the one that you would employ in an everyday or intimate setting. You're lying in bed, chatting with your partner about the people you just met at the dinner party. Your vocal tone is entirely different from the one you used in public; it's still your voice, being formed by your thoughts, but the way you use it is totally different. Most of the characters you play in film and television will be using their private voices, so to create those real characters you have to have flexibility in the quieter regions of your voice – the voice you use when talking about yourself, love, betrayal and all the other stuff you discuss with intimates. Historically, actors were trained to use the public part of their voice because most acting was in a very public arena where even intimate moments had to be projected. It can seem difficult, therefore, to reverse that logic and start using a more private vocal tone. But it must be your voice, centred in your vocal range. Basically, the character should sound like you.

If an actor reads for a part and gets it, I expect that actor to be using the same voice on the day of the shoot, not one that he or she has since concocted. By that I mean one outside their range or with the addition of odd affectations such as a lisp, or odd pronunciations. Anything, in fact, that the actor might have added to make themselves and the part a little more interesting, but which is not conveyed by the script.

Accents

If you have a slight accent, the director probably wants the character played with that slight accent. What is important is that you play the character's needs and wants clearly. What sort of accent should this character have? If you are unsure, ask the director: all being well, they will say 'Yours!' If the production company wants you to do a role in an accent that isn't native to you, don't lie and say you can do it when you can't, ask for help. Most will employ dialect coaches. I know that getting work is tough, and the temptation in any interview is to say, 'Oh, my grandfather was Irish, I'll be able to do the accent easily!' But don't just try to muddle through on a wing and a prayer: it'll be you up there on the big screen. Get the accent wrong and people will just think you're a bad actor. Nobody will say, 'What was that production company doing, not giving that actor a dialect coach?' They'll be saying, 'They couldn't even get the accent right!'

My advice, therefore, is to stick to your own accent. Being able to do an RP (Received Pronunciation) accent is useful too when required – so is developing a convincing American accent. So much film work is now in America that a good accent will always be an advantage. Not just a generalised American accent of the sort we often hear on British television, but a specific accent from somewhere on that great continent. Try not to pick the Deep South, or one of the rarer accents like Bostonian, but perhaps go for East Coast or West Coast. An easy way to do this is to pick an American actor who has a voice similar to yours in tone and pitch. Listen to them and study the accent.

So find, and then only use, your real voice.

Recently, on hearing the advice on voice that I was giving, an actor enquired, 'Are real actors needed at all?' When I asked her what she meant, she replied, 'Once you take away accents and the way we change our voice, what have we got? You can't do much with your body.'

Actually, you can do a lot with your voice and body without resorting to accents, distorted body shapes, or funny voices. There are, of course, actors who, with the aid of make-up and prosthetics, can produce great comic performances – one thinks of Eddie Murphy and, to lesser extent, Jim Carrey – but what the modern industry wants from the actor is an honest portrayal of the character, not for the actor to put another impressive notch on their acting belt. Impressive as some actors' work is, unfortunately it is clearly 'acting'. The truth is that both the public and the industry are now demanding much more.

Voice Production

The business of voice production deserves exhaustive study in its own right and as this is a book about screen acting – and there are many available about vocal technique – I'll keep it brief and to the point. But I recommend to any actor that regular voice lessons, especially around sight-reading, are an invaluable asset.

This simple rule should apply to all your preparation: Thought – Breath – Speak.

Sometimes your thoughts will be spoken, sometimes not. If you don't speak, the breath is just released. Imagine that your character is being insulted but has promised someone else that they will not react, no matter how angry they become. Every insult draws a mental response from you but you can't say it out loud. The result is a series of sighs, as the breath gathered for your verbal retaliation is dispelled without sound. Your character's thought process drives their breathing. The character's voice is governed by your breathing, which is why you must be able to relax properly. As soon as you start to feel stressed, the voice starts to tighten, the throat muscles stiffen and your jaw clenches. Your mouth is especially important in revealing your character's emotional state, and if there's any tension in that vital area around your lips, this will be lost. Your tension is literally disabling you from truly inhabiting the character.

So what sort of preparatory voice work should the aspiring screen actor do? The first essential is a daily routine of voice exercises, and the first of these should be finding your tone through relaxed breathing.

Exercise: Focusing Your Tone

Find a quiet spot to sit. Relax your body and focus your mind on centring your voice.

Take a breath and hum a single note. The note that you choose instinctively should be just below the middle of your range. Now take another breath and hum that note again, only this time a tone higher. Take another breath, hum the last tone and this time let the note go on a journey. Make sure you are humming at the front of your face, focused into the area around your eyes.

Take deeper breaths and make each hum last longer. Do this for at least five minutes, keeping your face and neck free from tension. If you feel your head jutting forward or your shoulders riding up, use this simple exercise from Alexander technique. Imagine you're a marionette, and a string is being pulled from the top of your head. As it is pulled up, your neck lengthens and your chin presses back into your throat. All your limbs are running off this single energy source.

Now hum a simple tune, 'Somewhere Over the Rainbow' perhaps.

You have now focused your voice into your facial mask.

Now take a breath and count to ten out loud.

Repeat, pitching your voice higher and higher with each number until you get to ten. This should be as high as you can go within your vocal range. Make sure the numbers are spoken and not sung, so that the note is not sustained.

Exercise: Diction

Tongue-twisters are great exercises for the tongue and lips.

Try saying: 'Red leather, yellow leather,' as quickly as possible, twenty times.

Try: 'Articulatory agility is a desirable ability, manipulating with dexterity the tongue, the palette and the lips.' Say that twenty times, again as fast as you can.

There are hundreds of tongue-twisters; discover which work best for you and practise them every day for at least five minutes.

Tips for Voice

- Use less volume but retain clarity and diction.

- Speak at the volume the microphone can hear you. Your voice only needs to reach the mic on the boom pole.

- In wide shot, the voice should be at the speaking level you would normally use to reach the people you are speaking to.

- In mid-shot, the voice should reach three or four feet away.

- In close-up, the voice should reach your hand a foot from your face.

- To find the shot size, watch the boom operator test the edge of frame. The microphone will hang just there.

- When using radio mics, or whenever you are unsure of the frame size, ask the DoP or the 1st AD. Do not ask the director.

- As the frame size gets smaller, reduce your vocal level accordingly, even though you might be repeating physical movements exactly.

- If you are shouting in the wide, keep the intensity for the close-up.

- If you're in doubt about your vocal level, ask the director.

- Naturalism – mumbling, breaking up lines and so on – is no substitute for a fully realised character.

- 'Less voice' does not mean whispering. If you find yourself doing that, recentre your voice.

- Vocal attack: the character's intention is carried through the word.

- Do not be tempted to do a vocal impersonation of someone. *Be* that person.

- In tracking shots, talk fast and walk ten per cent more slowly.

- Always do a warm-up before going on set, especially in the mornings.

- Use your own voice. No affectation or invention to make the character interesting.

- Keep continuity of your vocal levels within the scene. Shout where you shouted, whisper where you whispered every time.

- The character's 'private' voice is the one you will use most.

- Use your own accent wherever possible. Be wary of doing another accent unless the production company is supplying a dialect coach.

- The viewers want to see your character, not your acting.

Casting and Interviews

Casting is a process that actors really need to understand, and that many are confused about. Certainly it's the subject most of the actors I work with want to talk about. So to understand how it all works, perhaps we'd better start with the production process and work logically toward the first casting session.

Once a production company has 'green-lit', or given the go-ahead to a film or television series, they will begin the casting process almost immediately. On a big project, of course, the star casting would have been central to the project's being given the green light in the first place.

The first step is for the production company to break down the script to see how many and what type of locations and actors they'll need, and from this to make a quick calculation of how much the film will cost. Let's say the cost will be £10 million. If they spend that sum, they have to get their money back by selling it to various distributors, who will release the film in their own territories. This could be anywhere in the world, but in reality the big film territories are North America, China, Japan and Europe. To tempt buyers in these territories, the company reckons they will need a star actor – one they can afford, bearing in mind that such an actor's fee could be anywhere between £1–20 million. This fee, however, is 'above the line', which means it's above the actual cost of making the film. The company should be able to recoup this through the sales to other territories. 'Above the line' also means the cost of the talent needed to make it, including writers, directors, and other actors.

'Below the line' means the cost of physically creating the movie.

In television there's another complication, in that they have to assess the kind of attention a drama or its particular star will attract, so that the broadcasters can sell advertising around it. Once a company have committed to a script, the casting process begins.

Casting Breakdowns

The casting director will create a breakdown for every character in the project. This will include the name of the character, their age – sometimes generic ('forties' or 'twenties'), sometimes very specific – and a brief physical description: 'beautiful', 'tall with penetrating blue eyes', or 'a small dumpy man, bald and short-sighted'. This is followed by a short summing-up of the character, and these vary in detail depending on the size of the part. For a long-running television series, the breakdown could run to a full page and include a considerable backstory.

Once this has been finalised, copies will be sent out to selected agents, usually beginning with those who represent actors who have registered an interest in playing the leading parts. However, most agents will obtain a breakdown from one professional outlet or another.

Your agent will send the casting director your name, your Spotlight photograph and your CV. These days, of course, they'll more likely just send the casting director a link to your showreel online. Your CV should list your most recent credits, plus a round-up of earlier work. Most directors and casting directors are only really interested in your work in the last few years, although I remember a very good actor handing me his full CV: five pages of single-spaced type.

Even the casting process is controlled by economics. The production company has to hire meeting rooms, arrange to see the actors, have assistants on hand to greet and phone everybody, and even if they take submissions online, each one still has to be looked at, all of which takes someone's time. Self-taping has become endemic within the industry as it enables casting directors and production companies to see hundred of actors for every role. Self-taping will absorb a lot of your time, and it has become a bit of a burden to many actors, but you have to take it seriously and do the same amount of preparation on the text as if you were auditioning 'live' for the role.

Once the submissions start to arrive, the casting director draws up a list of possible candidates for the director to see. Usually, this will also include the names of actors the director has worked with previously.

These actors are then called in. Sometimes a large group of actors are seen together and the occasion put on tape to be watched later by the director and casting director. This is a popular method, not just because it allows more actors to be seen, but because they are also less nervous, and because the director gets to see them on screen right from the beginning. You might be asked to record your own reading of a scene, and most actors do this on their phones. Some, however, will do it on a small digital camera, and then send the casting director a link.

If I were to show the casting brief of our fictional film to a dozen people, I bet I'd get a different idea from each one as to who would be right for which part. That's why casting is so crucial from the director's point of view, and so frustrating from that of the actor, who of course can automatically see him- or herself in the part.

The director has to balance many conflicting things. I might meet an actress who is absolutely perfect for the lead in the film but she hasn't done much film work, just lots of television. Can I risk it? Will the producers let me?

Life on Screen

There's a true story about producers wanting to sack an actor, and it happened on the hit movie The Godfather. *It was only because the director, Francis Ford Coppola, was so stubborn and so sure of what he wanted that Al Pacino wasn't sacked from the original* Godfather *film. The producers couldn't see what Pacino was doing: they thought for such an important role he was too watchful, too passive. With each week of shooting that passed, they become more frustrated and angry, and they were on the verge of taking the decision out of Coppola's hands when they saw the rushes of the scene where Pacino kills the police lieutenant. At last they saw what Pacino was capable of. But as Coppola pointed out, they didn't change their minds until Pacino's character did something positive and active. He'd been telling them constantly that Pacino was doing exactly what he wanted him to do, but they wanted fireworks. You see how easily producers can panic! If Coppola hadn't been so sure of his actor, or Pacino himself less confident, things might have been very different.*

The producers on Zulu *wanted Michael Caine sacked, too. Luckily for him and world cinema he wasn't...*

And just to settle any nerves, it's very rarely that an actor is sacked from a film. It costs a lot of money, and it upsets everyone.

Understanding Your Casting

First of all, take a look at the things that cannot be changed:

- Your height.
- Your body shape.
- Your type of voice (high or low, gravelly or staccato?).

What about your general appearance – not your clothes or your hairstyle, though they are important, but what you see when you look in the mirror? Most of us don't like the shape of our nose, our lips are too thin or too big, our eyes are too small and our skin is covered in imperfections. Chins are always too weak or too prominent. Everyone has a catalogue of things that they don't like about their appearance. Don't judge yourself by your imperfections; as an actor they will probably serve you well.

Try to categorise yourself in the basic way that a casting director might. Discover your type. All actors have a type, and it will be with you until you achieve stardom and are able to get your pick of the parts. Until then, accept that you will always be associated with a type. If you are tall, with a deep voice, you will more than likely play authority figures – police or army officers, and so on.

A woman I know is a great singer and very eccentric, but if you saw her on the street you'd think she was a doctor. That's what she looks like. The way we look affects how people perceive us. We are all told not to judge a book by its cover, but in reality nearly all of us judge a person within moments of meeting them. Their class, their job, their character may turn out to be different from what we first thought, but that first impression will be our strongest, at least until we get to know them a lot better. Remember that most casting sessions last between ten and twenty minutes. The director and casting director will only get a first impression, so make it a good one.

So what do you see in the mirror?

'I'm a short fat man who looks like a car salesman.' 'I'm a pretty but not beautiful woman who looks like she works behind the counter at Boots.' 'I'm a tall man who looks like an academic.' You get the idea. Look in the mirror: be honest and go with your first thought.

Now ask family and friends. Do not be offended, be grateful for their honesty and candour.

Next, look at photographs of yourself. Try not to go for those in which you are posing with friends and family, but look at the ones where the camera has caught you in an unguarded moment. If you have video footage of yourself, even better.

Now put together what you first thought about yourself and the things other people said about you, and sum yourself up in a quick sentence; a brief but gritty description. 'An accountant type', 'Lawyer type', 'Shopkeeper'.

Why am I insisting on these short, pithy and somewhat crude descriptions?

As I've said before, film is first and foremost a visual medium and you need to say a lot about a character quickly and without too much detail. It's not that casting directors want to be crude, but time is precious and often an important part with lots of complexity has to be broken down into function and type. The casting brief for a recent British three-part thriller went out with the villain of the piece described thus: 'Dark and brooding. A psychopath with a twinkle in his eye.'

Of course, in physiological terms that's nonsense. It wouldn't really help you play the part but it gives everyone a clear image of what's wanted: a threatening, brooding presence but not the sort of person who would frighten away the horses. A charmer, but capable of turning into a complete monster. I think the casting people got it right with their little potted description.

And just because casting directors employ these expressions, it doesn't mean that they want the parts played as crude stereotypes. Far from it; they want sophisticated and well-researched actors who will bring the characters to life. It's just shorthand to ensure that everyone around the table –

producers, directors, casting people – is singing from the same song-sheet.

Even then it's subjective. As we all know, my idea of beauty might not be yours.

Your qualities

Every actor has a particular quality. Think about Tom Hanks, for example. He seems likeable, trustworthy, honest and decent, or at least those are the roles he excels in. He's a fantastic actor, but cast him against his essential quality and he's not quite so good. In the mid-eighties he was cast as the lead in *The Bonfire of the Vanities*, playing a greedy, arrogant banker who considers himself one of the masters of the universe. It wasn't exactly a success, not entirely because Hanks was miscast but that was certainly one of the reasons. Now think about Russell Crowe. His qualities are temperamental, tough, angry. Again, a fantastic actor when cast for those essential qualities, but when he's cast against type the results, although always professional, are nowhere near his best. And Cate Blanchett. Her qualities are an ethereal strength; she is a powerful woman. Perfect for playing Elizabeth I, Galadriel in *The Lord of the Rings*, or Katharine Hepburn in *The Aviator*, but those qualities didn't work so well when she was cast as a compromised teacher in *Notes on a Scandal*. It wasn't that she was bad in the role, in fact she was excellent. It's just that her inner qualities didn't quite chime with the part.

What are your essential qualities? That is, what qualities do you radiate? What would a stranger think of you? What would someone who's known you for years say about you? Ask enough people and you will get a range of opinions. Which other actors are you most like? Not just physically, but those who share the same range of qualities. Watch a lot of film and television and try casting yourself in various roles. You'll soon see patterns emerge, recognising actors who are playing 'your' parts. Try to describe their essential quality and casting type, then check out their careers on IMDb. You will see their line parts. Those are the sorts of parts you should be going for.

For example, Russell Crowe has played a lot of troubled policemen. Either they are corrupt or, more often, his character is a lone man fighting corruption. He's essentially the anti-hero: although his character does heroic things he doesn't appear to be a hero. Tom Hanks plays the ordinary person thrown into extraordinary circumstances and then, after an initial struggle, triumphing. Think about *The Terminal*, *Cast Away*, *The Green Mile*: a true hero despite his essential humility.

Once you understand your casting potential, you'll know which parts you should be going for and which qualities you should emphasise when being interviewed for a part. But remember that over the years your casting type and quality will change. Keep looking in the mirror, and keep watching your work on screen. Much better to be clear about parts you are right for and focus your attention on getting those.

Interviews

Most people think that you 'audition' for roles in film and television. You don't. You interview. And interviews can vary widely. Sometimes you'll be asked to look at a scene before you arrive, in which case your agent or the production company will email you the 'sides'. Sides can be a printout of the whole script, a number of scenes, or perhaps just one.

The casting director might tape your reading of the scene, or perhaps you will just be asked to read it. Either way it's best to learn it beforehand. Learning it means that, if the scene is taped, you won't just be staring down at the script. Anyone viewing the tape will then be able to see your face and understand your thinking. Even if it's not being taped, having learned it means you're less likely to make any silly slip-ups.

Everyone is nervous at interviews, but don't let the nerves swamp you so you stop listening. The director or casting director will give a brief summary of the project, and then a summary of the part they are seeing you for. Listen to the way they frame the character. What words do they use to describe them? 'He's a lovely bloke...' 'A bit of a bastard...' 'She's funny in a kooky way...'

I once heard a casting director say, 'He's the type of man who reads *The Economist* at the kitchen table!' Try to build what they are describing into your reading of the part. When they say 'She's funny', what they are hoping for is that that character will lighten the whole thing. So try to make the character funny in a real way: that is, play the reality but push it a bit, as you would with all comedy. This is also why it's important to learn the script, because once you've learned the words, you have the flexibility to adapt your reading.

Remember to play each moment of the script. The people reading in the other lines will not necessarily be very good, in fact they are mostly pretty dry and might sound bored, having read the same scene twenty times already. Ignore their reading and concentrate on what you discovered when you learned the dialogue. Break every scene down; be clear about the narrative. Is there a major change in the scene? If there is, play that conflict. As the great Alfred Hitchcock said, 'Drama is like life with all the boring bits taken out.'

What the casting director, director and producer want to see is that you have grasped the essential drama of the scene. Too many actors fall into the trap of reacting to the scenario in the room – relaxed, somewhat bored, with lots of gossipy chat. Do not mistake that for what they are really after.

Practise sight-reading at home. Read at least one script a day – there are lots available on the internet. The more you practise, the more confident you will feel.

Ask yourself:

- Where have I come from?
- What do I want?
- What is at stake?
- What is my emotional state at the beginning of the scene? What is it at the end?
- What is the function of my character?
- What world am I from and how do I fit into the one created by the writer?

The more work you do on the sides, the more choices you will have in the reading, and the more relaxed you will be. You won't be staring at the pages, hoping not to trip on a line. Having imagined where they have come from, how they sound, how they move, you'll be able to give your character a purpose, an objective.

If you make a mistake, admit it and ask to go back to just before that point. Most interview scenes are quite short so you shouldn't have far to go back. Don't panic and don't over-apologise. Lots of actors make mistakes on set. What they want to see is that you have the confidence to carry on.

Even if you don't get that job, a lot of important people will have seen your interview and will remember you. It often happens in this industry that bigger chances come with a second or third interview with the same people. You might get called back for another part in the same series.

Remember, 'Leave excellence in the room', and no one will forget you.

Self-taping

A casting director might ask you to learn a scene, shoot it on your phone and send it back to them. Generally they'll want it within a couple of days at most. Self-taping like this has become the favoured process for casting, mainly because they get a good impression of you in the part, but it's also quick and, since they don't have to hire rooms, comparatively cheap.

Tips for Self-taping

- Choose an interesting background. Although you'll be told that this doesn't matter, a well-chosen background will always make the scene look better.

- The camera loves depth, so don't do the scene with your back to a wall. Sit well away from the wall or find a background that has natural depth, like a window.

- Get some light into your eyes. The eyes are indeed the windows to the soul. In screen work they're vital for revealing your thought processes. If you have time, try to arrange lighting but if not, position a small piece of polystyrene or card, white side up, to bounce light into your eyes.

- You might be given a solo speech, but more often it will be a duologue. If so, try to get another actor of the right sex to read in the other part. This will give you a more muscular reading to work with.

- Do it several times and choose the best one. You only have one chance to make a first impression.

- Once it's been sent, try to forget about it. If they want you they will contact you. Do not badger your agent.

General interviews

Sometimes you just go for a general interview with a casting director. This is usually one who has a good relationship with your agent: it's in your agent's best interest for you to be seen and the casting director always wants to see new possibilities, as they never know what film or television series might be coming along next.

As with individual interviews, turn up early, look smart and be polite. And make sure that you know your CV – you'd be surprised how many actors don't bother to learn their own. When you ask them what they've been doing recently, they start sifting through their memory and mumbling about one job they did, then remember another they did just before that… Unfortunately, all this reveals is complacency and a poor memory!

Mention your most recent jobs, and talk about your relationship with the director and the other actors. Always be positive. Never bitch about the last job. If something you did recently hasn't been a success, make light of it, perhaps hint that there were problems and move swiftly on. The casting director will admire your discretion as well as your positive outlook.

Create an interesting impression of your career, showing how you've progressed, and emphasising those directors and production companies that you've worked with more than once. This will show that you are reliable and popular. Try also to let your personality shine through. Directors (and other actors) like actors who are easy to work with and will get along well in a company.

Now practise. Here's a set of standard questions you're likely to be asked. Get a friend to be the interviewer and film yourself. When you watch back the results try not to be too critical, but ask yourself what you could have done better, then do it again.

Try answering the following questions:

- What have you have been doing recently?
- Where did you train?
- Could you tell me something about your background?
- Have you been to the theatre or the cinema recently and seen something you liked?
- What have you seen on television recently that you have liked?

The point is to give the interviewer a clear and positive picture of yourself. As you talk about your work, try to flesh out the facts with interesting stories. Talk about people and things that happened. This will help you lead the interview in the direction you want. Also, try to ask the casting director questions so that you can get a feel for their likes and dislikes. Don't ask too many questions or the interview will be about them and not you, but try to make it a proper conversation.

If you only have a small list of credits, or even none at all, do not be tempted to lie. It's a small industry and if you tell even a small fib and get discovered, everything else on your CV will be in doubt.

Emphasise your training, or recent courses that you have done – the classroom work, your teachers. Talk about what you like and what you want to do in the industry. Do not give the casting director a long list of acting jobs you've been up for and not got.

Try to stay positive and relaxed. You are an interesting person and you are unique. No one else is quite like you. And remember that these people have given up their time to see you, so you must have something they like. And if you can, let yourself be amusing. If you make the interviewer laugh, they will be more inclined to remember you.

Tips for Interviews

- Be professional. Look smart. Dress as the character would but still look like yourself. I was once at a casting where the brief said 'early thirties, good-looking, sporty'. One actor turned up in white shorts, tennis shirt and a sweatband. He looked ridiculous and, frankly, desperate.

- Turn up at least five minutes early.

- Greet the director and any others in the room with a friendly smile. Some might shake your hand, most don't.

- Be smart and polite – not obsequious.

- Be relaxed and breathe calmly.

- If you get the chance, learn the script in advance.

- If you haven't had the script in advance, read the scene carefully. Identify the beginning, middle and end and try to find the moments of change. What is your character bringing to the scene? How are you like the character?

- Learn your CV.

- If you've had the pages of script in advance, try to find things about the character and their background that resemble your own. Talk about your own life and experiences honestly.

- Listen carefully and take on board what the casting director and director are saying about the character.

- Even if you feel the interview hasn't gone well, always leave with a positive attitude.

Adverts

Adverts are a valuable source of income, and they're being made all the time. The casting, however, can be speedy and very unnerving.

On arrival you'll be asked to fill in a form and then you'll be given the script. When you enter the casting suite you will be introduced to the director, who will tell you to stand on a mark in front of the camera. They may or may not introduce you to the others in the room, who will be the producer of the ad, the main casting director, and clients from the company whose product or service the advert will be promoting.

You'll be asked to say your name and that of your agent into camera, and then asked to show your right and left profiles. Just turn to your left for a moment, then to the right, then turn back to face the camera. Sometimes you might be asked to show your hands. Hold them up, showing the backs of your hands first and then your palms. The director will then talk you through what they want you to do.

Again, listen carefully. All the clues to getting the part will be there in what the director says.

And remember that most adverts are only thirty seconds long, so you have to speed up and really emphasise what you're doing. Suppose you're asked to take a sip of a drink and show that you're enjoying the taste. You have no thinking time: it's a quick sip and an instant reaction. If you are asked to look at something, really look at it. Don't just swivel your eyes and glance, but turn your head and look. What reaction do they want? If you're not sure, ask. For instance, you're standing at a bus stop and the car that's being advertised goes past. What should your look communicate? It might be envy, lust, anything. Whatever it is, try not to comment: however strange the request, just do it.

That's it. The director will thank you for coming, and you'll leave. Smile, thank everyone present for seeing you, and go. Never try to ingratiate yourself by talking about the advert or the product itself.

Conclusion

Final Tips

I said at the start of this book that the key ingredient for success as a screen actor – by which I mean you give convincing, compelling performances, rather than earn millions and win an Oscar (though that would be nice too!) – is to have screen-acting technique and a process. Hopefully this book has explained and informed you about that process, and given you useful exercises and ideas you can explore to increase your chances.

But of course it's not all you'll need to get work. Here are some of the other personal qualities you'll need in abundance…

Commitment

If you want to succeed you will have to commit yourself completely. It's not a part-time job. You may have to do other part-time jobs just to get by, but never forget that your real job is acting.

Positivity

It's hard remaining sensitive and open when you are rejected at almost every turn. But every actor is rejected. It's how you deal with it that's important. I've seen really good actors simply hide away from seeking work. They say they want work and are constantly moaning about their agents, but they do little themselves to create work. Subconsciously, they are withdrawing from the pain of rejection. Perhaps they secretly think that they aren't very good. Even star actors are terrified of being 'found out', fearing that one day someone will tap them on the shoulder and say, 'Sorry, you simply can't do it!'

Every day you have to remind yourself of why you want to be an actor. What is it you have to give? Be positive. Remember that you are unique. No other human being has had your experiences, your insights, and your genius in bringing a particular part to life. That is what you have to give, and never forget it.

Proactivity

Every actor has to be proactive in finding work, or even creating it. Write to directors and producers, make sure your details are circulating, and make sure that you stay visible in this very crowded marketplace.

Technique

Do theatre work wherever you can. Screen acting is always reinforced by stage acting: I believe it helps develop and strengthen your acting muscle. Remember that, in both screen and stage acting, you are inhabiting a character living in imaginary circumstances, created by a writer. The only difference, and it's a profound one, is process.

Stage acting is linear and organic. You all go into the same room and go through the rehearsal process together. You have your performance coaxed, developed and shaped by a skilled theatre director. But film and television acting is non-linear and non-organic.

Self-confidence

You meet the director at the casting, and then most probably you won't meet again till the day of the shoot. You prepare the part totally alone; you don't even know the other actor you'll be working with until you meet on set.

This demands a lot of self-confidence. You have to know yourself but also not be afraid of revealing yourself completely within this mechanical process. You also need a creative imagination and the ability to enter an imagined world completely, developing a character from a few words on a page. You'll have to stay relaxed in the middle of one of the most stressful, time-pressured environments ever invented, be able to stay concentrated after eleven exhausting hours of stressful filming, and stay focused when the crew are looking at their watches, willing the minutes to pass, and you still have your big close-up to come.

Stay prepared

> 'Luck is what happens when preparation meets opportunity.'
>
> *Seneca*

You need to be tenacious and totally focused on what you want– you'll also need some luck. Stay confident in yourself and of your talent, and work hard at your daily schedule of work, sight-reading, concentration exercises, constant observation of the people around you. Most of all, stay optimistic and stay happy.

Good Luck!

Remember, that next phone call could be for the meeting that will change your professional career. So stay ready, be prepared…